PROJECT ADVISER
DULI YANG TERAMAT MULIA
PADUKA SERI PENGIRAN BENDAHARA
SERI MAHARAJA PERMAISUARA PENGIRAN MUDA HAJI SUFRI BOLKIAH

CREATIVE DIRECTOR
HUSSIN BIN AHMAD

PROJECT CONSULTANT
CHIN TENG TENG

EDITORIAL DIRECTOR
NICK WOOD

CHIEF PHOTOGRAPHER
TARA SOSROWARDOYO

HOST PHOTOGRAPHER
HAJI KAMALUDDIN PDP HAJI ABU BAKAR

WRITER
JOHN FALCONER

PHOTO CO-ORDINATION
BRUNEI PHOTOGRAPHIC SOCIETY

PROJECT EDITOR
PETER SCHOPPERT

PROJECT MANAGER
SHAMIRA BHANU

A project of Brunei Shell Group of Companies.
© Brunei Shell Group of Companies, 1993.
All rights reserved. No portion of this book may be reproduced, in any
form and by any means, without the express written consent of the
copyright holder.
Published by Editions Didier Millet Pte Ltd, Singapore,
with Malay edition translated by Hj Khuttub Deen Mohd Abdullah
and edited by Rasiah Halil.
Colour separation by Colourscan Co. Pte. Ltd., Singapore.
Printed by Tien Wah Press, Singapore.
ISBN: 981-3018-03-8

ABODE
OF
PEACE

BRUNEI

DARUSSALAM

CONTENTS

**FOREWORD
BY HIS MAJESTY
THE SULTAN DAN YANG DI PERTUAN
NEGARA BRUNEI DARUSSALAM**
11

ABODE OF PEACE
12

NATURE'S GIFT
42

A LIVING HERITAGE
58

A RULER'S BOND
114

**TODAY'S PROSPERITY
TOMORROW'S PROMISE**
140

APPENDIXES
197

B i s m i l l a h i r   R a h m a n i r   R a h i m

I note that 25 leading photographers from the region were present in Brunei Darussalam. We welcomed them as our guests to witness and experience for themselves the way of life of the Brunei people in various aspects, including the culture, custom and traditions which have become our pride and practice for hundreds of years until the present day.

From that experience, which also involved 50 talented local photographers, has come this essay in the form of photographs of our country. We regard it as a historical source of great beauty, which has been created and arranged in that form to record the various events and happenings which have taken place here. This collection will remain forever as a testimony which speaks eloquently of those events and happenings of that era for generations to come.

It is on this basis that I am pleased to write these few words for this book.

Sultan Haji Hassanal Bolkiah

ABODE OF PEACE

دارُالسَّلام

Sunset. The sparkling water slapping softly against the wooden hull of a water taxi reflects the lights of the water village, Kampong Ayer, perched on a forest of slender stilts on the far side of the Brunei River. Smoke drifts from food stalls cooking *nasi goreng*, wafting an aroma of spices and chili on a gentle dusk breeze. Young girls elegantly dressed in *baju kurong* hold hands in placid family groups that amble past stalls selling betel nut, green bananas, jungle vegetables and papaya. As the time for Maghrib prayer approaches, the mellow sound of the *mu'ezzin* echoes through the moist tropical air and devotees converge on the mosque, clad in shimmering Malay dress interwoven with gold and silver thread, their heads capped by velvet *songkok*.

The scene could have been lifted from the pages of a 16th century account of Brunei Darussalam. But the electric lights and television aerials betray a contemporary scene. This is now. Today's fathers proudly leading their young sons to pray are only steps away from modern glass-sheathed office blocks that resonate with the amplified voice of the *Bilal* calling the faithful to prayer. In sophisticated offices, they spend the day in front of computers analysing data from international financial markets, projecting oil demand or formulating investment strategies. This is modern Bandar Seri Begawan, the capital of Brunei Darussalam.

From their tinted high-rise office windows, they can see across the choppy waters to Kampong Ayer, instantly recognisable in a 150-year-old watercolour by John Drinkwater Bethune, one of many travellers to visit Brunei Darussalam through the centuries. If Bethune could travel forward through time, he would recognise the same relaxed lifestyle of a century ago in the water village, where groups of smiling children splash below walkways, or fly kites in front of neat homes garlanded with pink bougainvillea. He would breathe a familiar atmosphere redolent with the contentment and warmth that pervades these close-knit communities

whose unspoken values of sharing, loyalty, filial respect and courtesy are as essential to life as the submerged foundations of the water village homes. Those values, entwined in the teachings of Islam, are fostered from birth, beginning with the first words whispered in a new-born baby's ear: "Allah is most great…"

This holy verse, which has greeted new-born Bruneian babies for generations, is one piece in a mosaic of common experience that shapes the country's strong community spirit. Villagers all lend

a hand to build a new home for a family, just as their ancestors did. Relatives, friends and neighbours will flock to a child's circumcision ceremony, and the intricate ritual of a wedding draws well-wishers from all over the country.

The family life that keeps grandchildren, children, parents, grandparents, cousins, uncles and aunts under one roof is as strong today as it was then. At meal-times, eager children still wait respectfully for their grandfather to join them before starting to eat, and at Hari Raya Puasa, following the fasting month, sons and daughters of all ages bend low to kiss the hands of their parents and ask forgiveness. But perhaps the essence of Bruneian life is captured most eloquently in the simple act of shaking hands. This everyday ritual finishes with a delicate touch of the fingertips to the breast, emphasising a heartfelt greeting.

All these things Bethune would have recognised in 1845 as he made his first brushstrokes of Kampong Ayer. But then there is much in Brunei Darussalam today that would have bewildered him and this is the key. So much has changed, yet so much has stayed the same. The pulse of continuity reaches back through to the early days of the country's rich, 1,000-year past and it has remained strong even in the last 150 years, when the country experienced a

WITH EFFORTLESS GRACE, A FISHERMAN CASTS HIS NET INTO THE PLACID WATERS OF TASEK MERIMBUN (PRECEDING PAGES), WHILE LENGTHENING SHADOWS SILHOUETTE A FATHER AND SON MAKING THEIR WAY TO EVENING PRAYERS ALONG THE WOODEN WALKWAYS OF KAMPONG AYER (LEFT). TRADITION PERMEATES MODERN LIFE ALSO IN THE WEARING OF THE *TUDONG* (HEAD COVER) AND IN THE ISLAMIC GREETING OF CLASPED HANDS, WHICH ENDS WITH A DELICATE TOUCH OF THE FINGERTIPS TO THE HEART.

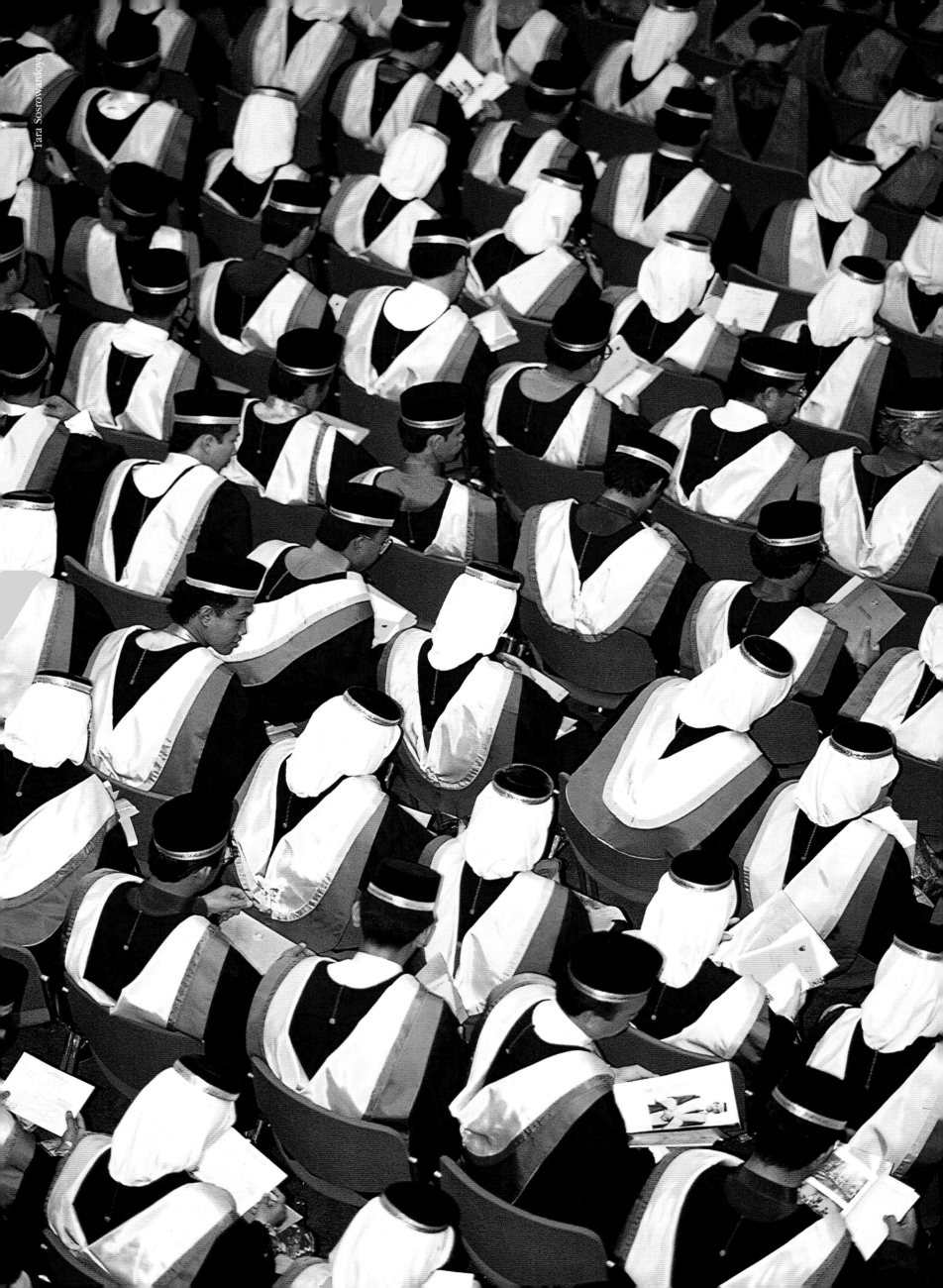

dramatic swing in fate. Brunei Darussalam's fortunes could hardly have ebbed lower during this period, when much of its territory was seized by land-grabbing foreign powers which threatened its very survival. But survive it did and today is enjoying a renaissance, the modern-day equivalent of its sixteenth century glory, when it held sway over an empire stretching from the Philippines through the whole of Borneo.

Then its wealth and power was based on trading camphor. Now, the wealth comes from other natural resources, oil and gas, which have transformed the country's fortunes in less than a single generation. Today, Bruneians enjoy one of the highest living standards in the world in one of only 10 countries without a national debt. It has been achieved by putting oil and gas earnings to work through development and investment. Foreign earnings from the Brunei Investment Agency now rival those from oil and gas and the rewards today include free education, a university, free healthcare for all, subsidies on staple foods, a national airline with growing intercontinental links, and a national television station — all without personal taxation. The country's health system is the match of any in the world, and includes mobile clinics and flying doctors who serve areas too isolated for road and river to penetrate.

As today's modern Bruneian climbs smartly-suited into a late-model car for the rush hour drive to air-conditioned offices in the downtown business district or the commercial and industrial suburbs, he knows that his country's present prosperity and future fortunes hinge on outside trade and taking a global perspective. But he also knows that ultimately, fulfilment depends on looking inwards — a wisdom instilled through the generations and one that lies at the very heart of the rule of His Majesty Sultan Haji Hassanal Bolkiah, the Sultan and Yang Di-Pertuan of Brunei Darussalam.

As the 29th ruler in an unbroken 600-year royal dynasty that is the oldest in South-east Asia, the Sultan more than anyone understands this philosophy which stems from a bedrock of shared experiences and values rooted in the uniquely Bruneian concept of *Melayu Islam Beraja* — Malay Muslim Monarchy. This national identity places the Sultan as sovereign leader, guardian of the faith and symbol and protector of Brunei Malay culture and explains the profound and indivisible bond between the Sultan and his people.

For most Bruneians, the unity of Sultan and subject is hard to describe because it is not a question they ever ask themselves. Like Islam, it is simply a way of life. A former chief minister, Pengiran Setia Negara Pengiran Haji Mohamad Yusof, who is also a member of the august ranks of nobility, puts it succinctly: Without the Sultan there would be no *rakyat* (people) and without the *rakyat* there would be no Sultan, he said. The two cannot exist independently.

Reminders of that deep bond come from the complex traditions embracing the Sultan and the royal family. To witness the coronation of the Sultan in 1968 was to flit back hundreds of years in time and see life breathed into an ancient and unique tradition. A Bruneian coronation is an event laden with symbols: the *Kris Si Naga*, which symbolizes the transfer of power from one Sultan to another; the heavy gold crown; the *Kuching Emas* (Gold Cat) that rests at the Sultan's feet; and the *Tongkat Ajai*, the golden hand on which he rests his chin. The longevity and complexity of this tradition is unique in South-east Asia. It is a powerful link to the past and a source of pride to all Bruneians who themselves still live within the social framework of a multi-layered hierarchy established through the generations, determining lines of authority and protocol based on status and age.

Today, the framework remains strong though a tilt towards greater informality has blurred formerly crisp distinctions as Bruneians have adapted to the swifter pace of modern living. An example is the change in meaning of the

honorific *Awang*, now used as a respectful preface for any male without royal links, the equivalent in Europe of 'Mister' or in Malaysia of *Encik*. The title used to be used only by descendants of a Bruneian noble family. Evolving to meet new challenges, Brunei Darussalam, with its long and volatile history, has absorbed influences from all over the region and beyond, including Johor, Java, Britain, Sumatra, China and Arabia.

The Sultan has balanced old and new and his modern style of leadership interlaced with tradition is best demonstrated at the thanksgiving ceremony in conjunction with the Silver Jubilee celebrations of the Sultan's accession to the throne. The Sultan arrives amid a colourful gathering, many wearing the traditional *jong sarat* while carrying the latest in video technology. The air is one of festivity rather than formality and the roads leading to the Taman Haji Sir Muda Omar Ali Saifuddien in the centre of Bandar Seri Begawan are lined with schoolchildren clutching the national flag.

In line with tradition, the Sultan's arrival is followed by formal greetings and prayers but it is the personal relationship of the monarch with his subjects that forms the central purpose of the visit. For nearly two hours the Sultan

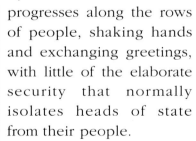

progresses along the rows of people, shaking hands and exchanging greetings, with little of the elaborate security that normally isolates heads of state from their people.

In the international realm, the Sultan has established a reputation among world leaders as head of a country with an independent spirit dedicated to peace and self-determination. He is as much at home speaking out at the Organisation of Islamic Conference as he is attending meetings of the Non-Aligned Movement or summits of the heads of state of ASEAN (the Association of South-east Asian Nations). Whether piloting his own jumbo jet or presiding over a cabinet-style Government in which he is also the Prime Minister and Minister

of Defence, he is the image of a progressive, modern ruler. But behind his modern approach lies the accumulated experience of one of the longest unbroken royal lines in the world. The Sultan has often stressed the importance of this past, notably in his inaugural speech to the United Nations, when he said his country had learned the realities of the world through generations of "peace but also war; wealth but also poverty; energetic commerce but also isolation; development but also exploitation; self-government but also foreign rule".

And it is the modern era that has heralded a period of change as important as any in the country's history. The Sultan, following in his ancestors' footsteps, has skillfully guided his country through this transition, integrating strands of tradition into a balanced approach that takes nourishment from the past while looking forward to the future.

Throughout its history, one of the country's strongest stabilising influences has been Islam. Brunei was one of the first South-east Asian nations to adopt the religion in the 14th century, acting as a guide to both personal conduct and state policy. The Sultan as spiritual leader responsible for fostering and safeguarding the faith has bequeathed to the nation the *Mushaf Brunei Darussalam*, a gilded handwritten *Qu'ran*, a copy of which has been given to every Bruneian household. He also launched an ambitious programme of mosque building, finest of which is the new Waqaf Mosque at Kampung Kiulap, a resplendent building with mosaic arcades, turquoise roofs and magnificent gold domes and minarets. The Sultan has also instigated the *Tabung Amanah Islam Brunei* (The Brunei Islamic Trust) and he opened the Islamic Bank of Brunei (IBB), two major national financial institutions which eschew *riba* (interest) and operate on lines permitted by the dictates of Islam.

Every year thousands of Bruneians join other Muslims in Mecca for the Haj pilgrimage. The Brunei international airport becomes a crowded theatre of emotion once a year, when relatives

ISLAM IMBUES AND PERMEATES EVERY ASPECT OF NATIONAL AND DAILY LIFE, AS SEEN IN THIS PHOTOGRAPH OF PRAYER BEADS, AND A DEVOTEE PERFORMING PRAYER ABLUTIONS IN THE OMAR ALI SAIFUDDIEN MOSQUE. THE SULTAN (RIGHT) IS SEEN AT PRAYER, WITH, ON HIS RIGHT, HIS ELDEST SON PENGIRAN MUDA AL-MUHTADEE BILLAH, AND ON HIS LEFT THE SULTAN OF JOHOR AND DR MAHATHIR MOHAMAD, PRIME MINISTER OF MALAYSIA.

gather to welcome back their loved ones returning on special charter flights from their sacred journey to the Holy City.

Other living examples of the central role of Islam in all walks of life include the widespread use of the Jawi script on shopfronts, letterheads and posters, the commemoration of important events in Islamic history, the use of the Islamic calendar and the emphasis on religious education in schools and colleges with scholarships to Al-Azhar University in Cairo, and other top Islamic institutions. This continuing relevance of Islam and its interlocking role in the Malay Muslim Monarchy concept is graphically mirrored in the architecture and landscape of the capital. By day the golden dome and cupolas of the Omar Ali Saifuddien Mosque form the central dominating feature of the skyline, echoed in the rooflines of the Istana Nurul Iman, the principal residence and workplace of the Sultan. The mosque and palace overlook both the new and old — the commercial centre, on which future prosperity depends, and the thriving Malay community of Kampong Ayer, symbolising the traditions which determine the shape of that prosperity.

Appropriately, it was at the heart of this scene, at Taman Haji Sir Muda Omar Ali Saifuddien, ringed by mosque, palace, commercial centre and Kampong Ayer that Brunei Darussalam celebrated one of the most important days in its history. On 1 January 1984 the words "Allahu Akhbar..." (God... Almighty!) rang out in the rain-swept square and the country took its place in the world as a fully independent sovereign state on the international stage. The Sultan chose to launch this new era of progress and development with a reaffirmation of a commitment to tradition and shared values by stressing the indivisibility of the country's full title, 'Brunei Darussalam' (Abode of Peace). Though known to much of the world until then simply as Brunei, the country has been called 'Darussalam' for generations, the word appearing prominently on the nation's

600-year-old crest. Thus, in the full glare of world publicity, this link with the past also became a symbol for the future.

The moment has been described by the Sultan as the greatest of his reign and his feelings reflect those of his people who speak with pride of the occasion. For the thousands of Bruneians standing on the damp grass in the floodlit square, the sense of continuity was heightened by the voice of the man entrusted to call out those first words, the Sultan's father, Sultan Haji Omar Ali Saifuddien, who had made the first steps along the road towards independence as Sultan until his voluntary abdication in 1967.

The responsibility then passed to his son, who in his maiden *titah* delivered soon after his accession, emphasised that continuity:

"With Allah's will, I shall also continue and always safeguard and maintain in earnest the efforts to uphold the true image of Islam and the customs of Brunei..."

A SULTANATE'S ANCIENT GLORY

Brunei Darussalam's traditional fishermen are probably among the few to see the approaches to the capital as experienced by generations of merchants and ambassadors who, through the centuries, came to trade with the Sultanate. From the wide expanse of Brunei Bay, the river curves towards the capital with richly wooded hillside descending to the water, often beneath the dramatically-changing skies so typical of the area. Apart from a polka-dot of modern villas on the hillside, little can have changed since Brunei Darussalam's early capital was founded on these wooded slopes. Almost invisible from the river, and a little below the Brunei Museum at Kota Batu are the remains of that capital, indicating human habitation dating back as far as the eighth century, one of the earliest sites in South-east Asia. Here are to be found the remains of a royal palace with a large pavilion overlooking the river, the sole pre-European stone buildings found so far in

THE ROYAL REGALIA FORM THE MOST POTENT LINK WITH THE COUNTRY'S TRADITIONAL HERITAGE. HERE A YOUNG SULTAN HAJI HASSANAL BOLKIAH IS SEEN WEARING THE CEREMONIAL CROWN DURING HIS CORONATION IN 1968. THE CROWN IS SHOWN IN CLEARER DETAIL (RIGHT). THE CEREMONIAL *KRIS SI NAGA* IS ANOTHER IMPORTANT ITEM OF THE REGALIA, AND IS WORN BY THE SULTAN TO SYMBOLISE HIS NEW AUTHORITY.

Borneo. This archaeological site alone attests to the longevity and significance of Brunei Darussalam's history. From the 14th century, the country's history is clearly defined. Before that is the shrouded darkness of pre-history only fitfully pierced by shafts of light — scattered references, brief tantalising glimpses of shifting fortunes and the burgeoning power of a nation that was destined to become one of the major forces in the South-east Asian region.

From earlier references it is clear that the country was of considerable importance both as a trading and military power. Of all the exotic produce gathered in Brunei for export — musk, tortoiseshell and cowries, aromatic woods such as sandal (*laka*) and *gaharu* — none was in greater demand than camphor. Gathered by forest dwellers and sold to merchants on the coast, it was traded all over South-east Asia and as far afield as India, though the finest went to China where it commanded fabulous prices.

By the ninth or early 10th century P'oni, as Brunei was known in Chinese texts of the period, was described as the best source of camphor in the world. In 977, Poni's envoys to China were lavishly received. Like the oil and gas industry of today, the wealth created by camphor financed the development of a powerful state whose traditions and regalia were admired by contemporary chroniclers. Such was the country's fame that the name Borneo appears to have derived from Brunei and until the late 19th century, Brunei's capital was known as 'Borneo Proper'. By the 11th century Brunei was a place of wealth and strength. An account published in 1225 by Chau Ju-Kua, Inspector of Foreign Trade at Fukien, China, reported that the 'king' went abroad with an escort of 500 men armed with double and single-edged swords and wearing cuirasses of cast bronze. Chau noted that domestic implements were made of gold, and the *kain jong sarat* worn by the wives and daughters of the rich were "melted gold-coloured silk". He also described the 'king' as possessing more than one hundred warships. Other contemporary accounts list nine vassal states paying homage to Brunei during this period, among them Sulu.

Although the great 13th century traveller Marco Polo never visited Brunei, he was well-acquainted with its fame, and his writings include several descriptions culled from contemporary accounts. All attest its power, its trade in spices and the great number of merchants who visited the country. Polo even asserts that the Chinese emperor envied the wealth of Brunei and would have liked to have conquered the country.

This early empire had its roots in the geography of Borneo and was defined by the Malay social structure that evolved to govern it. The jungle-cloaked, hostile terrain meant rivers and the sea formed the arteries of trade so it was inevitable that centres of power and commerce were concentrated at river mouths, just as they are today. By controlling the trade between the interior and outside world, these centres grew in wealth and prestige and so Brunei evolved, with the authority over watersheds handed down by the Sultan either to members of the royal family, pengirans, or as private hereditary domains. The relationships with ethnic groups has stood the test of time, with different groups occupying historically-defined areas and engaging in particular occupations. Thus, Brunei Malays and other related Malay groups — the Dusun, Murut, Bisaya, Tutong, Belait and Kedayan — have historically been linked to the centre of court power, while trading and interacting with other groups such as the Penan and Iban, who reside further in the interior. Today

Entrance to the Brunai River — Aug 9

THE BRUNEI BAY LANDSCAPE HAS CHANGED LITTLE OVER THE YEARS, AND THIS WATERCOLOUR (BELOW) SHOWS THE VIEW AS SEEN BY ENGLISH NAVAL OFFICER EDWARD CREE, WHO VISITED BRUNEI DARUSSALAM IN 1845. THIS HISTORICAL CONTINUITY IS ALSO REFLECTED IN THE EXQUISITELY-WORKED JEWELLERY WORN BY A MODERN BRIDE-GROOM, AND IN THE DECORATED BRUNEI *KIRI* OR KETTLE (RIGHT), WHICH FOR CENTURIES WERE PRIZED AS TRADE GOODS THROUGHOUT SOUTH-EAST ASIA.

most Penan have opted for a more settled existence, such as the group at Sukang high on the Belait River, who live in a longhouse built with assistance from the Bruneian Government. The Iban, who started to arrive in significant numbers towards the end of the last century, also retain their communal long-house lifestyle while benefiting from the advantages of modern government.

Brunei's importance as a centre of trade was celebrated well beyond South-east Asia. Arab chroniclers also paid tribute to its commercial and military prowess and one of the earliest accounts was the *Ajaib al-Hind* or *Wonders of the Indies*. It describes the water city of Sribuza, which modern research locates in Brunei Bay, and writes of the floating houses of the town. Mention of the medicinal powers of the country's camphor was made by a celebrated Baghdad physician Ishak ibn Imran as early as 900 AD. Further details emerge from Abu Abdullah as-Sharif Al-Idrisi's *Book of Delights* (1154 AD). He records that Muja, as Brunei was called, was noted for the beauty of its women, with their hair worn long and tied around their heads with pendants. Ruled by a great king named Kamrun, its sailors were famed as sea rovers, who struck out fearlessly at their foes in ships commanded by pengirans wearing gold collars.

The country did not escape the attention of legendary Arab explorer Ibn Battuta, a man who surpassed Marco Polo in the range of his wanderings and from time to time in his tendency to embellish his accounts. He praised Brunei for its valiant warlike people, and for its abundant gold, silver and silk, and described the sovereign as the equal of the King of China.

Such wealth attracted envy and at some point in the 14th century Brunei fell under the sway of the Javanese Majapahit empire. For some 50 years its glory waned. But Majapahit in turn declined and renewed trading and diplomatic links with China saw a sharp turn in Brunei's fortunes. By 1408 it was held in such high esteem by China that when the Bruneian ruler died on a visit there, he was buried in great splendour in a tomb at Nanking.

Islamic links in Brunei cast back to the days of pre-history but it was not until the 14th century rise of Mughal rule in India that the religion became a crucial formative factor. Simple to follow in its main tenets, relating to individual conduct as well as the policy of the state, Islam made swift inroads into the crumbling Hindu empires of the archipelago. Bruneian historians have done much research, particularly at the Pusat Sejarah (Brunei History Centre) since it was set up in 1982, to establish a chronology of the Royal Family, and the Pusat Sejarah has published a family tree of rulers which collates surviving *Salasilah* to produce a definitive list. This dates the founding of Brunei's Islamic state to Sultan Mohammad Shah, who reigned between 1363 and 1402.

With the accession of Sultan Sharif Ali, also known as Sultan Berkat (1425–1432), the role of Islam was further consolidated. Sultan Sharif Ali, a descendant of the Prophet, built the first mosque in Brunei and established a judicial and legal system based on Islamic principles, which in essence continues to the present day. He is also credited with improving the Jawi script and introducing the crest, which today forms the central part of the national flag.

Since this time, Islam has been a constant factor in Brunei's history and the rest of South-east Asia. European imperialism has blossomed and died but Islam continues to strengthen. Perhaps the manner of its arrival had something to do with this for it was introduced not by the sword but peacefully along international trade routes. In the years before 1500, Muslim traders controlled many of the trade routes through the Middle East and India, down the Straits of Malacca to the South-east Asian archipelago to China. From the time of the Prophet, Muslims have often been traders, valuing the freedom of commerce as well as obeying the religious injunction to travel in search of knowledge.

The royal line descended from Sultan

The Town . Brunai — 'Vixen'   "Pluto"   Ne

The Sultan's Palace !!

Mohammad Shah began the new expansion of the Brunei empire, especially the fifth Sultan of Brunei, Sultan Bolkiah (1485-1524), whose achievements overshadowed those of his predecessors and many of his successors. He is revered as the ruler who oversaw the greatest flowering of Brunei's empire. Provinces in Sarawak came under his dominion, Sulu was re-taken and even Manila was briefly held with the aid of a huge cannon, *Si-Gantar Alam* ('He who shakes the world'). Legends abound concerning the exploits of this colourful character. A great sailor, he took with him on his travels the royal orchestra, earning him the title *Nakhoda Ragam*, the Singing Captain. It is said that he demonstrated the extent of his empire by taking a jar containing a *gantang* (eight pounds) of pepper on his travels, leaving a single peppercorn at each landing place until the stock was gone. He died at sea while returning from Java but his reign is commemorated in the carved tomb in Kota Batu that remains to this day a focus of veneration and prayer. During the month of Ramadhan, the *Qu'ran* is recited continuously at his tomb by readers who work in shifts and repeat the text some 40 times. The ritual is repeated at the Makam Di-Raja (Royal Mausoleum) where the Sultan's father and other Sultans are buried, emphasising again continuity and a strong regard for history.

The opening years of the 16th century brought other, ultimately less welcome pressures to bear on South-east Asia as foreign powers, greedy to exploit the riches of the east, disrupted trade patterns that had existed for centuries. First came the Portuguese capture of Malacca in 1511. Eight years later Ferdinand Magellan of Spain set sail in an expedition to explore a western route to the East Indies. After completing the first recorded crossing of the Pacific, Magellan was killed in a skirmish at Cebu but his two surviving ships put in at Brunei Bay in May 1521. Magellan's official chronicler Antonio Pigafetta gives a graphic account of the first encounter between the western world and the thriving splendid court of the greatest city in Borneo, then presided over by Sultan Abdul Kahar, who received them with warmth. Musicians played, and a *prahu* decorated with gold leaf and flying peacock feathers came to meet them. Eight of the Sultan's senior chiefs boarded the ships bearing presents of betel, fresh food and cloth and eight days later the Sultan granted them an audience. The tenor of Pigafetta's narrative is one of surprise at the magnificence and luxury of the Brunei court. He describes being mounted with his companions on two silk-caparisoned elephants for the procession to the palace, probably then at Kota Batu — a building surrounded by brick walls and fortress-like towers on which were mounted 56 bronze and six iron cannons. The audience chambers were adorned with silk hangings and had windows with brocade curtains.

Pigafetta paints a vivid picture of a trading empire at the height of its power with settled customs and governed by a ruler both stately and friendly, surrounded by a large retinue "all attired in cloth of gold and silk... (carrying) daggers with gold hafts adorned with pearls and precious gems". He also refers to a water village containing 25,000 families — certainly an exaggeration — and *padian* sellers carrying market produce from house to house by boat.

The visit ended in confusion and misunderstanding, however. Seeing a fleet of the Sultan's boats approaching their ships, the Spanish feared treachery and attacked, capturing a number of Bruneians who were later sold as slaves. In fact the Bruneian force had been gathered to fight a rival and had no hostile intent towards Pigafetta's group but the damage was done and this harsh repayment of hospitality sowed the seeds of a mistrust that was to bedevil relationships for succeeding generations.

As a large cosmopolitan centre, Brunei became a recognized focus for Islamic missionary activity, sending teachers to many islands including Mindanao. In 1576, Francisco de

THE CEREMONIAL SHIELDS (LEFT) USED DURING ROYAL EVENTS FORM PART OF THE AGE-OLD REGALIA. WHEN ENGLISHMAN FREDERICK MARRYAT VISITED SULTAN OMAR ALI SAIFUDDIN II'S AUDIENCE HALL IN THE EARLY 1840S, HE FOUND A CHAMBER ADORNED WITH SIMILAR SHIELDS, WITH THE RULER AND OTHER CHIEFS HANDSOMELY DRESSED IN SILKS, SATINS AND GOLD EMBROIDERY (RIGHT TOP). THE TRADITIONAL ARCHITECTURE OF KAMPONG AYER IS ALSO SEEN IN THIS VIEW OF THE ENGLISH BOMBARDMENT OF BRUNEI TOWN IN JULY 1846, AN ATTACK INSTIGATED BY JAMES BROOKE.

Sande, Spanish governor of the Philippines, wrote a worried despatch about this missionary activity and Brunei's power, followed up two years later by a successful assault on the Sultan, after he had refused to stop spreading the word. Much of the town was put to the torch, including its "sumptuous mosque, a very large interesting building, quite covered with half relief and gilded". The victory was fleeting as disease, and strong oposition from the Bruneians, forced the invading Europeans to withdraw. Sultan Saiful Rijal rebuilt the mosque, prepared new fortifications and trained a force of 1,000 warriors, and when the Spanish returned a year later, they were repulsed.

The Spanish attitude differed radically from the Bruneians, who were known for their toleration of other faiths. It is most vividly illustrated by the experience of Christian missionary Tradescant Lay in 1836, who discussed the relative merits of religions with nobles, including the Sultan himself. So interested was Sultan Omar Ali Saifuddin II that he several times invited Lay to live in Brunei, saying: "stop here, and I will give you a house and send to Europe for your wife". This tradition of religious tolerance continues today with the picturesque Anglican church of St Andrews ministering to Christians and several colourful Chinese temples serving the Chinese community.

The increasing grip of Europeans on the spice trade upset the balance of power in the region. Former vassal states such as Sulu broke free and Brunei suffered a period of civil war in the 1660s which ended only with the accession to the throne of Sultan Muyiddin in 1673. No further direct assaults were made on the country in the following two centuries until the arrival of the British in the 1840s. This marked the start of a tempestuous relationship that progressed from a struggle for control of Brunei's territories to a friendship between equals.

One day in 1845, Captain John Drinkwater Bethune, visiting Brunei to negotiate a location for a British settlement with Sultan Omar Ali Saifuddin II, looked down on Brunei Town

from a spot close to the present Ministry of Foreign Affairs. Sketching the scene before him, he mused on Brunei's glorious past and uncertain future. The view he drew of Kampong Ayer, easily recognizable today, was published under the title *Views from the Eastern Archipelago*, accompanied by a text from St John Spencer. Spencer wrote: "A city erected on piles and posts on the river might dwindle away all together and leave behind it no ruin…" and while the latter part of the 19th century was certainly a low point in Brunei's history, as its territories diminished and fortunes ebbed, Kampong Ayer continued to thrive. Above all, the country remained independent, almost unique in South-east Asia in never having become the colonial dependency of a European power. Instead, a strong and binding alliance blossomed with the British that the Sultan has acknowledged helped preserve Brunei Darussalam as an 'Abode of Peace'.

INDEPENDENCE PRESERVED

The man responsible for Brunei's 19th century reversal of fortune sailed up the Kuching River in the schooner *Royalist* in 1839 in search of trade. He was James Brooke, no ordinary adventurer but a man of almost missionary zeal driven by a vision of extending British influence throughout the archipelago. After helping Pengiran Hashim suppress a rebellion in Brunei's Sarawak province he managed to secure as his reward the governorship of the province through a combination of diplomatic manoeuvring and outright threat. In Brunei the economic situation was perilous and piracy rife because of the disruption of inter-island trading patterns by European incursions. Both elements left Brunei vulnerable and Brooke took advantage, dividing loyalties with offers of trade with some court elements, backed with protection against piracy and trade from the British Royal

THE PEACEFUL LIFESTYLE OF KAMPONG AYER AT THE TURN OF THE CENTURY IS EVOKED BY THESE EARLY PHOTOGRAPHS (TOP LEFT AND BOTTOM), TAKEN BY ENGLISH ARTIST AND WRITER A. HUGH FISHER AROUND 1908. TRADITIONAL STYLE IS ALSO BROUGHT TO LIFE IN THE EVERYDAY OBJECTS ON THIS PAGE — THE *CHALAK MAKANAN*, A WOODEN CAKE-MAKING MOULD AND THE *LESONG KAYU*, A WOODEN MORTAR USED FOR POUNDING CHILI AND OTHER SPICES.

Navy. Labuan was ceded to the British crown in 1846 and in the following years Brooke, and after his death his nephew Charles, encroached further and further into Brunei territory, exerting political and physical pressure to force the sale of provinces. When in 1881, British North Borneo was given a British royal charter to administer Brunei's northern territories in what is now Sabah, Brunei found itself squeezed between two land-hungry territories intent on snatching as much as possible. Such was the threat that one exasperated British colonial official remarked in the 1880s that unless the growing ambitions of these two neighbours were controlled "there will be not a pengiran left in Brunei".

Bitter resentment in Brunei spilled over into aggression in 1861 when an angry Pengiran Dipa Negara forcibly expelled Charles Brooke from Mukah. This determination was echoed by Sultan Abdul Mumin, who shortly before his death in 1885 made his pengirans swear an oath that no more lands would be leased to foreigners. Brunei forces were not strong enough to crush the White Rajahs in battle, so the Sultans adopted a skillful political game which, though it did not stop the shrinking of territories, did preserve the core of the nation and ensure its survival. The strategy in 1888 brought the Sultanate under the protection of the British who were by now uneasy about the ambitions of Brooke and the British North Borneo Company. Even this did not stop Charles Brooke, who in 1890 in his most outrageous move, seized Limbang, dividing Temburong from the rest of Brunei, a move disputed to the present day.

Brunei strengthened its protective link with Britain in the early years of the 20th century but it was not until the discovery of oil in 1929 that the country's fortunes saw an upturn, bringing in its wake great material wealth that once more set it on the path to regaining full independence. Brunei's progress towards its present prosperity took place under the tutelage of the present Sultan's two predecessors. Sultan Ahmad Tajuddin came to the throne in 1924 and presided over the first uncertain steps of the country's renaissance. His rule covered the discovery of oil and a growth in the country's material assets. He guided Brunei through the grim days of occupation by the Japanese in World War II, and oversaw the start of post-war construction.

On his death in 1950 he was succeeded by his brother, Sultan Haji Omar Ali Saifuddien III, who continued this work and launched an ambitious development plan to rebuild the country, putting to work its newfound wealth while remaining true to tradition and the dictates of Islam. Even when he voluntarily abdicated in 1967 and handed over the reins of government to his son, the present Sultan was able to take advantage of his father's experience during the long and complicated diplomatic negotiations which finally led to the resumption of full independence. On his abdication, Sultan Omar was given the honorary title of Begawan Sultan (Blessed Sultan) and the capital, Brunei Town, was renamed in his honour. Thus in the 20th century, as the British empire crumbled, Brunei's fortunes surged. Ninth century Brunei had depended on its natural resources, camphor and other jungle valuables, for its success and again it was nature that wrought a renaissance.

A NEW ERA OF DEVELOPMENT

In a computerised control room of startling sophistication, Rosli Haji Said calmly monitors the loading of the mammoth liquefied natural gas (LNG) tanker *Belanak,* moored more than four kilometres away. Rosli is one of the new breed of Bruneian technocrats who run the oil and gas industry, the source of 64 per cent of Brunei Darussalam's foreign earnings. He is based at the LNG plant at Lumut, which, since its official opening by the Sultan in 1972 (then the first project of its size and imagination in the world), has shipped more than five million

THE PRESENT SULTAN'S LATE FATHER, SULTAN HAJI OMAR ALI SAIFUDDIEN III (REIGNED 1950-67) IS SEEN WITH HIS CONSORT, THE RAJA ISTERI PENGIRAN ANAK DAMIT IN A PORTRAIT TAKEN IN THE 1950S (RIGHT TOP). ALSO IN THE 1950S, SIR OMAR IS SHOWN HOSTING MALCOLM MACDONALD, COMMISSIONER-GENERAL FOR THE UK IN SOUTH-EAST ASIA, IN TRADITIONAL BRUNEI STYLE IN THE ISTANA (RIGHT BOT-TOM). SIR OMAR'S DAUGHTER, PRINCESS MASNA, IS SHOWN AT A EAR-PIERCING CEREMONY IN 1954, WHILE SULTAN AHMAD TAJUDDIN, THE 27TH SULTAN OF BRUNEI (REIGNED 1924-1950), IS SEEN SPEAKING AT A FORMAL CEREMONY.

Peter Chen

tonnes of LNG to Japan annually. In 1993 the plant once again grabbed global attention when it completed a massive five-year rejuvenation programme, again an industry first, designed to see it through a second 20-year supply contract with its Japanese customers. Gas for the LNG plant comes mainly from the South-west Ampa field, one of seven offshore oil and gas fields that today supply 95 percent of all of Brunei's oil and gas exports. The offshore harvest is supplied through more than 200 permanent structures scattered across the South China Sea.

All the country's oil exports and its entire gas production is handled by the exploration and production company Brunei Shell Petroleum (BSP), owned jointly by the Government and a company in the Royal Dutch Shell Group. BSP is one of five companies in the Brunei Shell Group that covers the entire spectrum of the oil and gas industry. Brunei LNG, which runs the LNG plant is another, while Brunei Shell Tankers owns a fleet of seven LNG tankers plying between Brunei Darussalam and Japan. The tankers are leased to Brunei Coldgas, which buys LNG from BLNG and sells it to customers in Japan. The fifth company in the family is Brunei Shell Marketing which runs all the country's road and riverine service stations.

The oil and gas industry has catapulted Brunei Darussalam to prosperity in 30 short years. Shell was one of the first oil companies to search for oil in Brunei in the 1890s and was the only one to persevere in the early years of the 20th century after other companies had given up. Its tenacity was rewarded in 1929 when the Shell-owned British Malayan Petroleum Company discovered the poetically-named Padang Berawa (Wild Pigeon Field), later to be renamed the Seria field. The discovery started the transformation of a swampy area of south-west Brunei Darussalam, populated by only a few small villages, into a modern-day centre of industry liberally dotted with 'nodding donkeys' that still dip rhythmically to pump crude oil to the Seria terminal.

After the Government, the oil and gas sector is the largest employer and in line with the Sultan's drive for self-sufficiency has initiated a massive investment in education, with sponsored scholars sent to universities and colleges both overseas and locally. But the effort goes further than that. Training and development programmes for Bruneian contractors supporting the industry have improved not only the volume and scope of business kept in the country but also encouraged and prepared companies to diversify into other areas of growth.

Diversification is perhaps the Government's most important development goal to overcome the economic imbalance caused by Brunei Darussalam's reliance on oil and gas. The creation of a Ministry of Industry and Primary Resources in 1989 was an important move in the nation's plan to establish a long-term industrial and economic base. It brought under one roof the industrial unit, fisheries, agriculture, and forestry, all key areas for development.

One major step towards self-sufficiency has been large-scale cattle farming. Much of the country's needs are now met by its cattle station at Willeroo in Australia's Northern Territory, which has a larger land area than Brunei Darussalam itself. A number of other programmes have also been launched, establishing research stations and model farms and creating incentives leading to successes in dairy production, as well as increased yields in vegetable and fruit growing, and fisheries.

The story of oil and Brunei Darussalam are intimately connected, for oil is one of the oldest links with the past, representing a connection through the millennia with the land which has created this mineral wealth in the slow accretion of plant forms borne by the rivers and deposited on the seabed. This basic connection between land and prosperity is a reminder of the unique value of the natural environment, a value that increases yearly in direct proportion to the unceasing global destruction of natural resources and habitats.

BRUNEI DARUSSALAM'S OIL AND GAS INDUSTRY ENCOMPASSES A CRITICAL PERIOD IN THE NATION'S MODERN DEVELOPMENT, FROM THE 'NODDING DONKEYS' THAT HAVE RHYTHMICALLY PUMPED UP OIL FOR MORE THAN HALF A CENTURY (LEFT), TO THE COMPUTERISED SOPHISTICATION OF THE LIQUEFIED NATURAL GAS CONTROL ROOM AT LUMUT AND THE HELICOPTER SHUTTLE OPERATION USED TO FERRY WORKERS TO OFFSHORE PLATFORMS.

Since the dawn of history, Borneo has been a land of forests, and forests have been the source of her wealth. The camphor for which Brunei was renowned throughout Asia financed a prosperous empire and such was its mystique that the people of the interior who collected the precious gum spoke *pantang kapor* (the camphor language) while searching, in the belief it would not be found without this ritual. Camphor is no longer accorded such reverence but the forest contains other riches and secrets, only a small proportion of which are known today. While economic necessity and rapacious loggers have denuded much of South-east Asia's forest cover, some 70 per cent of Brunei Darussalam's rain forest is still untouched. It is good fortune that Brunei Darussalam with its oil wealth does not need to fell timber and this has fostered an appreciation of the beauty and scientific importance of one of the most magnificent rainforest environments of the world.

AN ANCIENT HERITAGE

The Batu Apoi Forest Reserve in Temburong is a dramatic introduction to the beauty of Brunei Darussalam. The journey from Bandar Seri Begawan to the rain forest takes only a few

hours by ferry, through a rich variety of ecological habitats. In this tidal maze, mangrove and nipah palm crowd the river's edge. The long aerial roots of the mangrove reach into the water and mud to act as a stabilising web, preserving from erosion mud flats teeming with crustacean and fish life that in turn are an important resource for Brunei Darussalam. The habitat, which survives in few other areas of the world today and is protected in the country, supports otters, the proboscis monkey, eagles, kingfishers and waders, as well as providing cutch, a dye used in tanning.

The ferry bursts from these sheltered tributaries into the broad expanse of Brunei Bay, a great sheet of water stretching off to distant cloud-capped mountains. Skidding in a long arch, the launch shoots up the Temburong River for the last leg to the district capital at Bangar. The Batu Apoi reserve, which is upstream, is flanked by densely-cloaked precipitous inclines, their summits overhead sheathed in mist. In the centre of the reserve is the Kuala Belalong Field Studies Centre, a neat cluster of chalets perched on the steep bank of the river just upstream of its confluence with the Temburong River. The project, instigated

by the Universiti Brunei Darussalam, is the most visible example of the country's commitment to conserving and better understanding the environment. The project's sponsors include Brunei Shell, and funding has financed a major research programme by the Royal Geographical Society to study a host of aspects of the forest environment, from water run-off and the formation of rivers to the social behaviour of ants, representing one of the most intensive examinations of the forest environment ever undertaken.

The knowledge gained will extend far beyond the management of Brunei Darussalam's own rain forests and have implications on an international scale. Education is an important facet of the centre, with the chalets catering for supervised parties of visitors from schools, Government departments and elsewhere. While scientists may appreciate the importance of the forest, it is only by direct experience of this unique environment that the layman can begin to directly understand its beauty and significance. Further opportunities to visit and explore this protected world will come through an outward bound school on the Temburong River, built by Brunei Shell Petroleum and sponsored by Shell International Petroleum Company. It is scheduled to be ready in 1994.

To stay in the forest is a unique experience. Here the great but shallow-rooted dipterocarps support their height with massive buttressed trunks, living a dynamic, interdependent existence of immense complexity with all the other plants of the forest down to tiny ferns and microscopic lichens. This shadowy, humid gloom, erupting from time to time in an

LIKE ANY MODERN CAPITAL, BANDAR SERI BEGAWAN BOASTS RAPIDLY EXPANDING COMMERCIAL AND RESIDENTIAL SUBURBS, SEEN IN BOTH MODERN HIGH-RISE HOUSING BLOCKS AND THE HI-TECH FACADE OF THE ABDUL RAZAK PLAZA (RIGHT). THE COUNTRY'S NATIONAL CARRIER, ROYAL BRUNEI AIRLINES, HAS ONE OF THE MOST MODERN AIRCRAFT FLEETS IN SOUTH-EAST ASIA, AND A REPUTATION FOR COMFORT AND EXCELLENT SERVICE.

explosion of colour as a butterfly flashes by, is the scene of an unceasing struggle for survival and dominance characterised by a swift opportunistic reaction to change: the death of a great tree, dislodged from its shallow roots and sent crashing down, allows a shaft of sunlight to pierce the gloom, the signal to saplings living a

half-life in its shade to fight for their only chance to occupy that small window of brightness. This constantly changing habitat also shelters a wealth of animal life, shy and retreating to the eye but evidenced by a barrage of screams, whistles, hoots and buzzing. Against the constant sawing of cicadas and other insects, the far-carrying and musical call of the dowdy, rarely-seen Argus pheasant echoes in the undergrowth, while the astonishing call of the helmeted hornbill has been most memorably described as a cry that "starts with widely-spaced poops, accelerates slowly to a loud climax of te-hoop notes and ends in maniacal laughter". Noisiest of all are the gibbons, whose wild whoops echo through the forest accompanied by the crash of branches as the troop swings through the treetops.

Kuala Belalong is only one element of a nationwide conservation effort aimed at protecting ecosystems. These areas have all been designated Protection Forests and Primary Conservation Areas, including the 48,000 hectares of Batu Apoi forest, the Sungai Ingei conservation area (18,500 hectares) and the Ulu Mendaram conservation area (6,200 hectares). Together with protected peat swamp and mangrove forest, the reserves represent both a responsibility and an opportunity. The forest's potential as a storehouse of beneficial plants, of new economic products, building materials or as yet undiscovered medicinal drugs has hardly been tapped. Brunei Darussalam knows better than most what that means because it was from these selfsame forests that camphor came, its main source of ancient trading wealth.

unset. In a quiet waterway off the Brunei River, silhouetted against a crimson skyline, fisherman Haji Sarbini prepares his nets in the bows of his small wooden fishing boat, watched by his 15-year-old son Hamid. It is a good time for fishing, Haji Sarbini knows, because he has worked on the river all his life just as his father did before him. His son, in contrast, is a modern schoolboy by any standards, fluent in computers, knowledgeable about international current affairs, concerned about the preservation of rain forests, and like any youngster, he enjoys visiting that symbol of world society, McDonalds.

Though Haji Sarbini's son and his contemporaries will form the future generation of Bruneians working for the continued progress and prosperity of the country, they remain indivisible from their parents and the past generations that have moulded the character of the modern Bruneian. From the first conscious moments after birth, Hamid has in a sense been preparing for his role as a member of his community. In morning religious school he studies the *Qu'ran* and learns about Islam as a way of life, and in afternoon history lessons he takes pride in the rich history of the country, as well as learning modern skills necessary for the future. Back at home that schoolbook history comes alive in a family life which is steeped in custom and forms the very core of society.

Hamid will be one of the next generation of Bruneians who, guided by the shared values of *Melayu Islam Beraja* — the very same values and traditions which sustained and nourished their ancestors over the centuries — will seek to apply them to a future based on progress, self-reliance, hard work and an international outlook.

In the fishing boat, neither father or son contemplates this vision of the future as Haji Sarbini sends his net hissing over the placid water with a deft flick of the wrist, to land with a scarcely audible sigh in a perfect circle. Both father and son represent the past and future of Brunei Darussalam — Abode of Peace.

THE TURQUOISE AND GOLD MINARETS AND DOME OF THE NEW WAQAF MOSQUE AND THE CURVED MALAY ROOFS OF THE ISTANA NURUL IMAN FORM AN APPROPRIATE FRAME FOR THIS AERIAL VIEW OF THE CAPITAL (RIGHT), WHILE THE LEGACY OF THE FUTURE IS CAPTURED IN THE FRIENDLY SMILE OF A YOUNG BOY, AND IN THE DEDICATION SHOWN BY A REFORESTATION PROGRAMME WORKER.

2

NATURE'S GIFT

Rio Helmi

S ince the dawn of history, Brunei
Darussalam has been an island of forests and today, more than
three-quarters of its natural forest cover is still intact. The
pictures opposite and on preceding pages show a dense and
impenetrable web of nipah palm and mangrove in the
Temburong district. In this scenic setting, a Bruneian heads for
home through the maze of estuarine creeks and small islands
that make up much of the country's coastal belt
(above). The barn swallow (overleaf, left) and
the redshanks (right top and bottom) are two
resident bird species that live off the food-rich
mud flats and mangrove swamps.

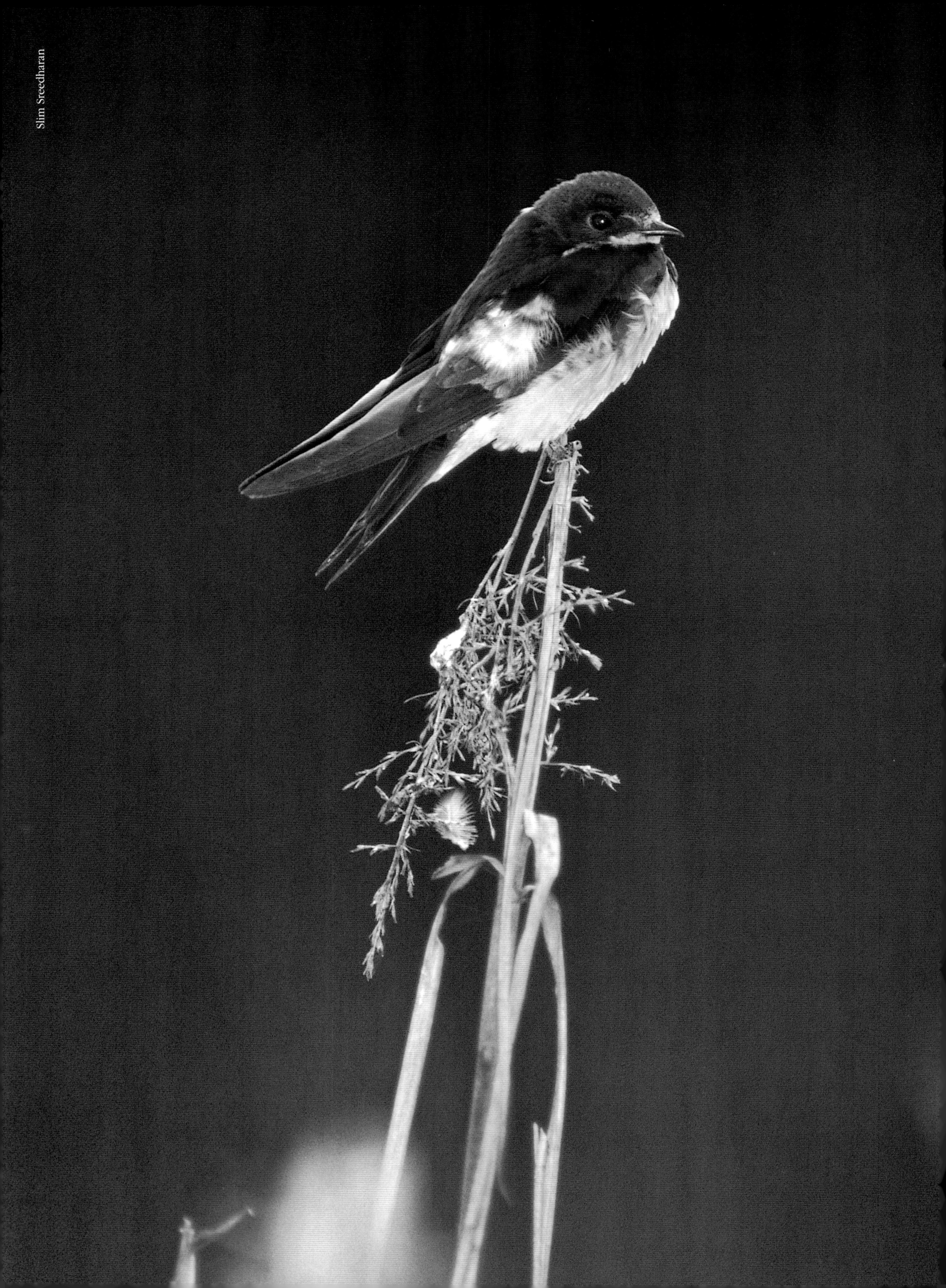

Slim Sreedharan

Slim Sreedharan

Slim Sreedharan

Rio Helmi

F urther inland from the district capital, Bangar, the Temburong River forms an ox-bow as it winds through primary dipterocarp rain forest (above), while the aerial view of Tasek Merimbun (left) reveals in dramatic perspective the glittering waters of this freshwater lake, a popular picnic spot for Bruneians twenty-seven kilometres inland from Tutong.

Mike Yamashita

B runei Darussalam's relatively
untouched forests also contain interesting geological formations,
as seen here in the dense jungles of Temburong (above
and right bottom), which are among the most beautiful
in Borneo, and studded with unexpected pleasures
such as this rushing waterfall (right top).

Desi Harahap

Duangdao Suwanarungsi

Pisit Jiropas

Slim Sreedharan

Slim Sreedharan

Pisit Jiropas

BRUNEI DARUSSALAM HAS A RICH ABUNDANCE OF PLANT AND ANIMAL LIFE. PROTECTED BY ACTIVE CONSERVATION POLICIES. ITS DENSE FORESTS ARE HOME AND REFUGE TO A WIDE RANGE OF CREATURES THAT INCLUDES SEVERAL RARE TYPES OF HORNBILL, AS WELL AS ENDANGERED SPECIES LIKE THE BORNEAN GIBBON.

Slim Sreedharan

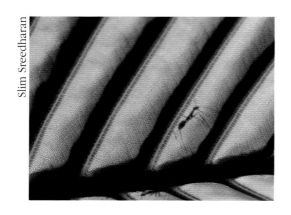

Pisit Jiropas

Gueorgui Pinkhassov

Duangdao Suwanarungsi

Pisit Jiropas

Duangdao Suwanarungsi

NATURE FORMS A COMPLEX WEB OF INTERACTING HABITATS, FROM THE SMALLEST CREATURES AND PLANTS TO THE DIPTEROCARP GIANTS OF THE UPLAND RAIN FOREST. BUTTERFLIES SUCH AS THE RAJAH BROOKE BIRDWING SHIMMER IN THE FOREST GLOOM, WHILE LICHENS AND EPIPHYTIC FERNS ADD THEIR OWN TRACERY OF DELICATE BEAUTY.

Slim Sreedharan

Raghu Rai

Mike Yamashita

A forest giant stands out starkly from the crowns of living dipterocarps at Temburong (left), home to the Batu Apoi Forest Reserve and the research-oriented Kuala Belalong Field Studies Centre. The heavy humid air of the forest (above) wreathes the trees in a soft blanket of mist, creating a scene of mystic beauty.

3

A LIVING HERITAGE

Ara Guler

Mike Yamashita

Religious instruction is an essential part of life, and young people receive tuition in all forms of religious practice. Pupils at the Religious College at Tutong (preceding pages) pray together, while a teacher (left) holds a Qu'ran-reading class. The generations come together in prayer in the Omar Ali Saifuddien Mosque (above), whose beautifully proportioned arches (overleaf) impart a sense of peace, as they are seen reflected in the ablution pool where Muslims perform the *wudhu* (ablutions) before prayers.

Gueorgui Pinkhassov

Gueorgui Pinkhassov

Much of the religious activity of the capital is centred around the magnificent Omar Ali Saifuddien Mosque, where the faithful gather in prayer (right). For some, the building is also a refuge from a busy world (above). One of newest mosques in Bandar Seri Begawan is the Waqaf Mosque, a resplendent turquoise and gold building completed in 1992, shown on preceding pages.

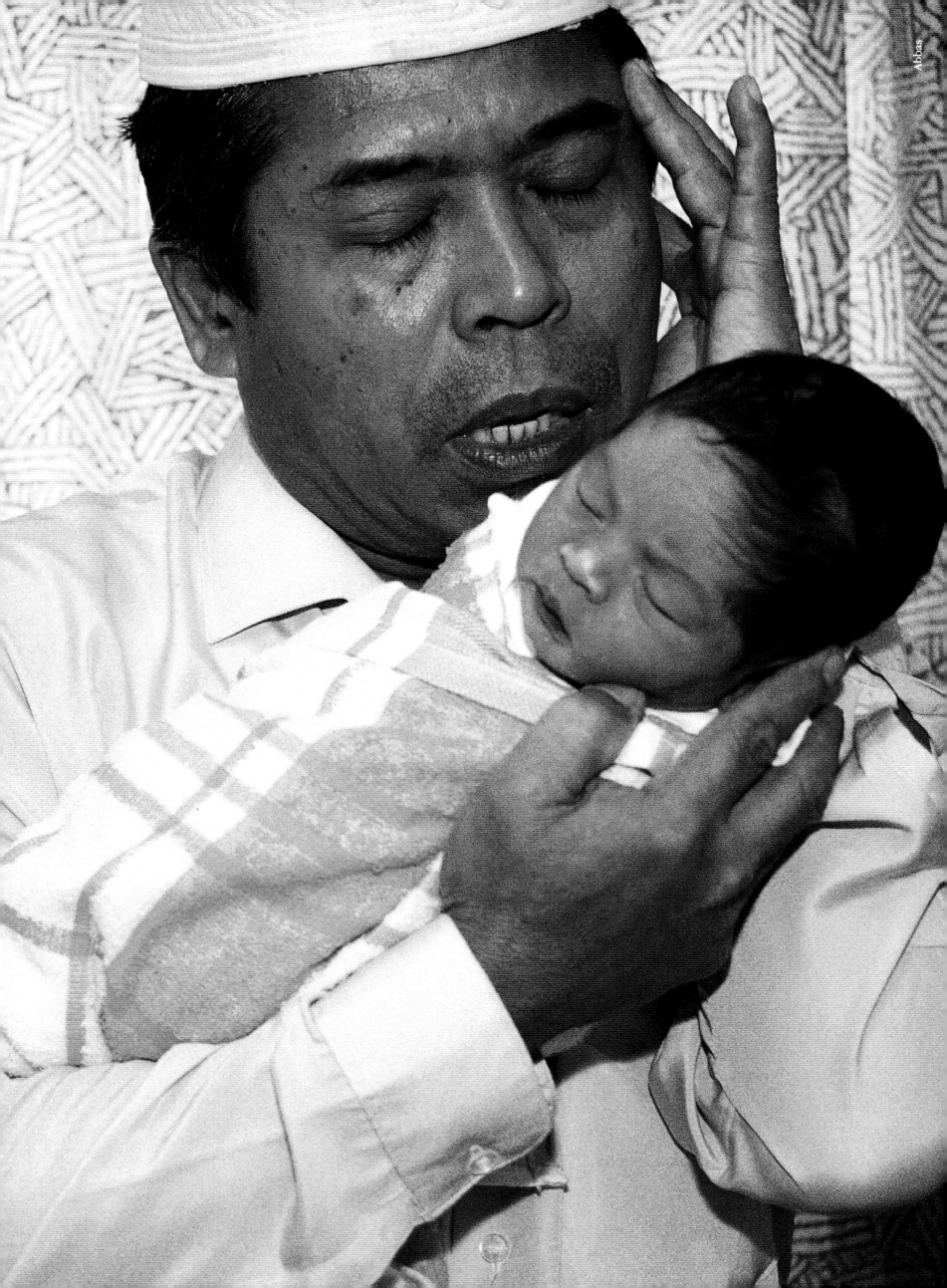

Mohd Yusof Mohd Yassin

I n an Islamic practice common the world over, a Bruneian child is introduced to Islam from the moment of birth, when the *azan* (call to prayer) is whispered into his ear (left). Thus, the first word the child hears is the name of Allah, coupled with a call to surrender to His will. The next important religious event is the *papat jambol* (above). Friends and relatives gather to shave the baby's head, give him a name and introduce him into the Muslim community in which he will grow up.

Hiroshi Suga

Muslims believe that when a servant of God marries, he perfects half of his religion, and in Brunei Darussalam this momentous step is marked with both solemnity and celebration. Here, the *kadhi* leads the solemnisation ceremony or *akad nikah* with the groom, in the company of male peers and relatives. The *kadhi* will seek the bride's consent to the marriage in a separate part of the house.

Wang Miao

Thanksgiving is an integral part of life for a Muslim, and prayers are performed at every occasion, from the ordinary to the significant. There are different prayers for different occasions, although the most commonly recited is the *suratul fatihah*. In the picture above, the *doa selamat*, or thanksgiving blessing, is being held to celebrate the marriage of a young man in Kuala Belait.

Gerald Gay

While the festivities following
the marriage ceremony may take many forms, ancient Malay
custom is at the fore of this Kampong Ayer wedding. Here the
hadrah players (above) chant in tune with their playing as
they lead the groom to the bride's house. At the wedding
feast itself, the entertainment can range from modern
to more traditional music, as represented by this
Kuala Belait musician (right), who has played at
weddings for more than 30 years.

Tara Sosrowardoyo

Leong Ka Tai

A girl (left) displays the traditional finery of a Bruneian wedding costume. The headdress is elaborately designed, from the *tajak* formed by layers of flowers, to the golden *sarbang* fastened around her forehead. Equally impressive is this bridegroom (above), dressed in a richly-woven suit and special ceremonial headdress or *dastar*. Seen here on the way to his wedding, he is accompanied by the *Pangangun* (left), a professional employed as a ceremony organiser and marriage counsellor.

Abbas

A newly-married couple are seated on a wedding dais or *plamin* in the bride's house as part of the *bersanding* ceremony (above). This is a cultural ceremony where the bride and groom, often in matching clothes, sit in state to declare to the world their married status. It is customary for wedding guests to be given a festive egg (right), a symbol of fertility. Tradition also survives in the rich and expensive gold brocade of *sinjang* and *jong sarat* worn by a guest, an ancient Bruneian craft which has been kept alive through the efforts of the Arts and Handicrafts Centre.

Munshi Ahmad

Leong Ka Tai

Hj Yacob Dato Paduka Hj Sunny

Dominic Sansoni

The skills and crafts handed down over generations reach perhaps their fullest expression in the modern Bruneian's love of traditional jewellery. Modern styles have drawn upon these cultural links, and any gathering, formal or informal, will bring forth an array of Bruneian designs, including beautiful *JONG SARAT* weaving (left)

Wang Miao

Leong Ka Tai

Tara Sosrowardoyo

T he power of living tradition
gives Brunei Darussalam its sense of identity, making it aware of
the past that has formed it and supplying a sense of common
purpose for the future. Shown here are weaving in
Kampong Ayer (above), a boat-maker shaping a *prahu
tambang* or water taxi (right, top), and a group of
musicians playing traditional music during
festivities in Temburong.

Gerald Gay

Mike Yamashita

Gerald Gay

In Brunei Darussalam, generations
of skilled craftsmen have adapted traditional skills to new uses.
Here a craftsman (above) works an intricately chased pattern
into a silver box at the Arts and Handicrafts Centre
workshop, while in Bandar Seri Begawan's Tamu
Kianggeh market, a stallholder (right) sells trimmed
palm leaves for making rice cakes or *ketupat*.

Gerald Gav

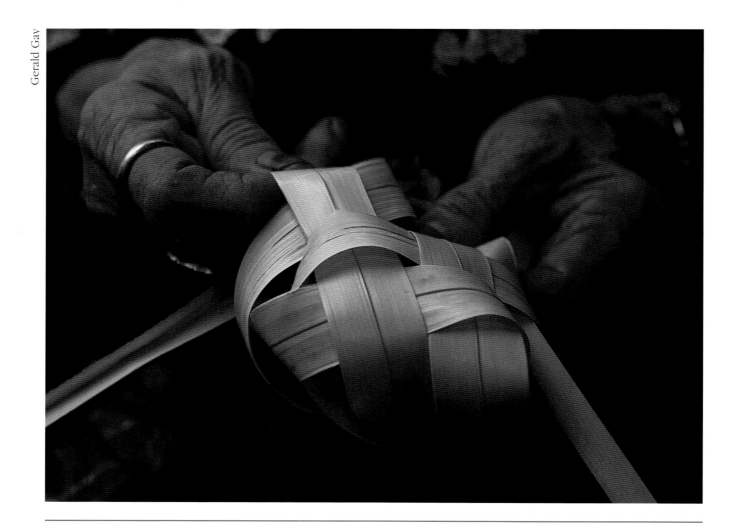

Nimble fingers deftly construct a *ketupat* case (above). This intricately-laced strand of palm serves as a handy container for rice. Boiled for many hours in the *ketupat* casing, the rice forms a kind of subtly-flavoured cake. A young girl (right) at the craft workshop at Berakas concentrates on stripping a length of rattan for making mats, or *tikar rotan*.

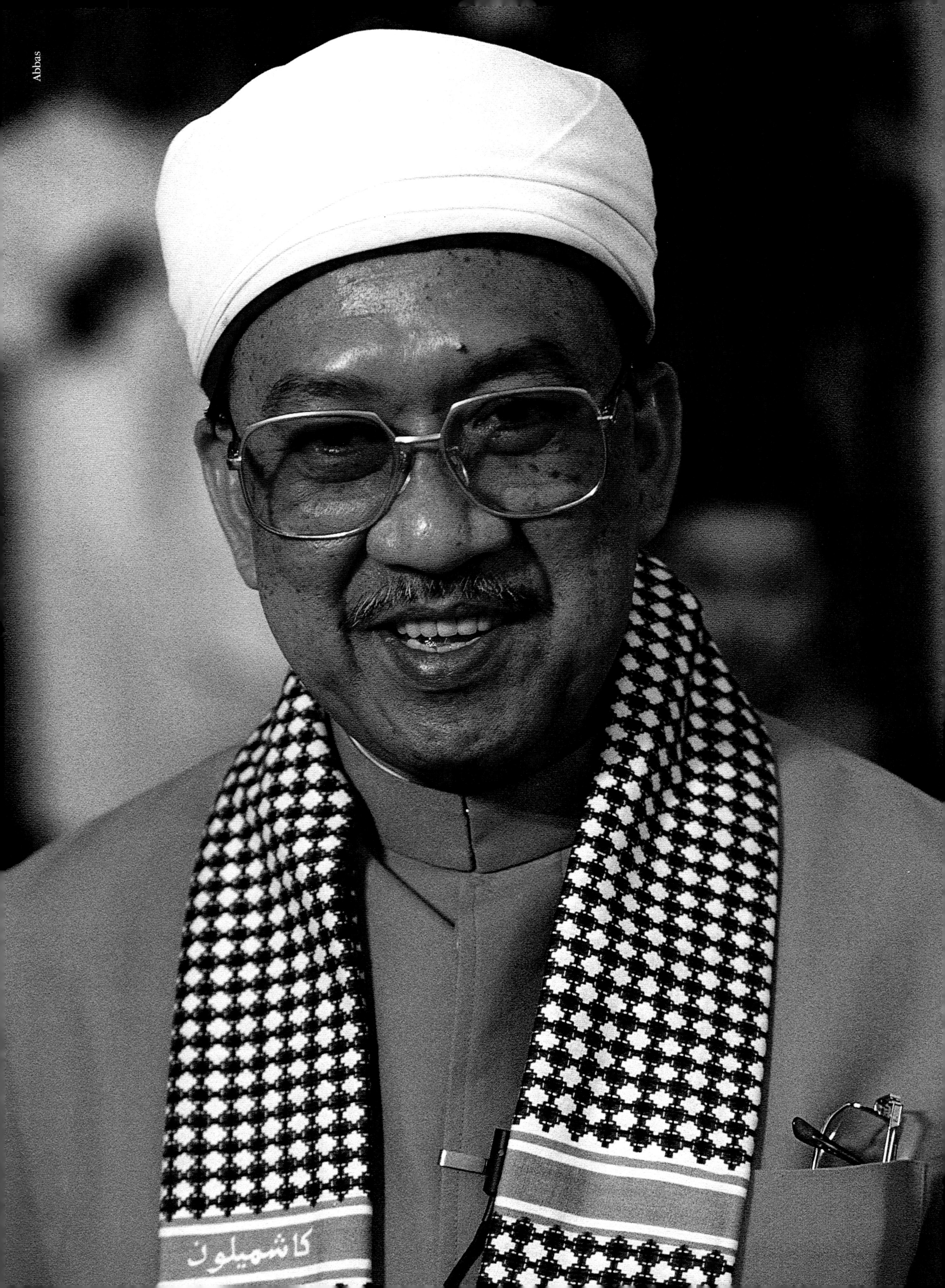

Abbas

Raghu Rai

T he solace and repose of
religion are captured in this quiet corner of the women's section
of the Tutong Mosque (above), during the noon prayer or
zhuhor. The religious life of Brunei Darussalam is exemplified in
the figures of its key officials, which include the Chief Kadhi of
Religious Affairs (left) and the Deputy Kadhi of Belait
District, (overleaf left), who is of a younger generation
of religious officials. Islamic law is administered by
the Shariah Court (overleaf right).

Tara Sosrowardoyo

Tara Sosrowardoyo

T he deepening twilight
emphasises what could easily be an age-old scene — two girls
strolling along the wooden walkways of Kampong Ayer
(preceding pages). The stilt houses are connected to the modern
part of the capital by water taxis. Above, an army officer
immaculately turned out in evening dress crosses the Brunei
River with his wife for an evening function at the
Istana Nurul Iman, while commuters returning
home at dusk (right) transform the Brunei River
into a busy highway. The mood quietens
(overleaf) as a fisherman leisurely fixes his net.

Gueorgui Pinkhassov

Living over the water in Kampong Ayer, with its intimately-styled wooden houses, heightens the close-knit sense of community which stems from generations of shared experiences. Here neighbours steal a moment from their myriad household chores to stop and chat through louvred windows.

Gueorgui Pinkhassov

C hildren linger along the maze
of wooden walkways that connects the houses of the water
village in a complex web of paths. The modern yet traditional
atmosphere of Kampong Ayer is reflected in this family scene
(overleaf), where the latest accoutrements of modern living
contrast with the timeless scene of a man fixing his
home. A boy late for school cycles along the narrow
thoroughfares beneath the dome of the Omar Ali
Saifuddien Mosque (following pages).

Dominic Sansoni

Religious tolerance is practised in Brunei Darussalam, and non-Muslim residents in the capital have their own places of prayer. A young girl (left) worships in the Chinese temple in Bandar Seri Begawan, while also in the capital, the minister of the wooden church of St Andrew's (above) offers Anglican services in a variety of languages.

Prince Haji Sufri Bolkiah

T he airy open spaces characteristic of Malay architecture are seen in this spacious living area in a house in Kampong Ayer (below right). Two women (above) lean out the window of a bamboo house in Kampong Parit, while (top right) is a Bruneian longhouse at Kampong Melilas in the Belait District. Home to the Iban, the standard longhouse design with verandah, a semi-private inner area and family rooms beyond has remained intact, while linoleum, fitted doors and windows indicate concessions to the modern world. Traditional crafts are very much alive in this longhouse, where weavers work on baskets (overleaf left) and food covers (overleaf right).

Wang Miao

Ara Guler

Wang Miao

Mike Yamashita

Wang Miao

Dennis Lau

Much of Brunei Darussalam's indigenous community is employed in the Government and oil and gas industry, but many still pursue their primarily agrarian way of life. A Murut woman brings in corn from the field at Temburong (top left), while the headman or *tuai rumah panjang* at Kampong Melilas (bottom left), a convert to Islam, breaks for lunch to cook his catch of fish over an open fire. Although the old method of processing sago (*ambulong*) at Kuala Balai (above), by trampling to extract the essence, has given way to more modern production methods, sago still forms the basis of Bruneian culinary specialities.

Dennis Lau

F ree education exists for all citizens of Brunei Darussalam. Here among the scenic splendour of the forest at Rumah Kampong Melilas, accessible only by boat, children make their way to school dressed in the traditional *tudong* (left). The Penan, another small community in Brunei Darussalam, has also adopted a more settled lifestyle, as seen by this woman feeding her pet hornbills at the *rumah panjang* or longhouse at Kampong Sukang (above).

113

4

A RULER'S BOND

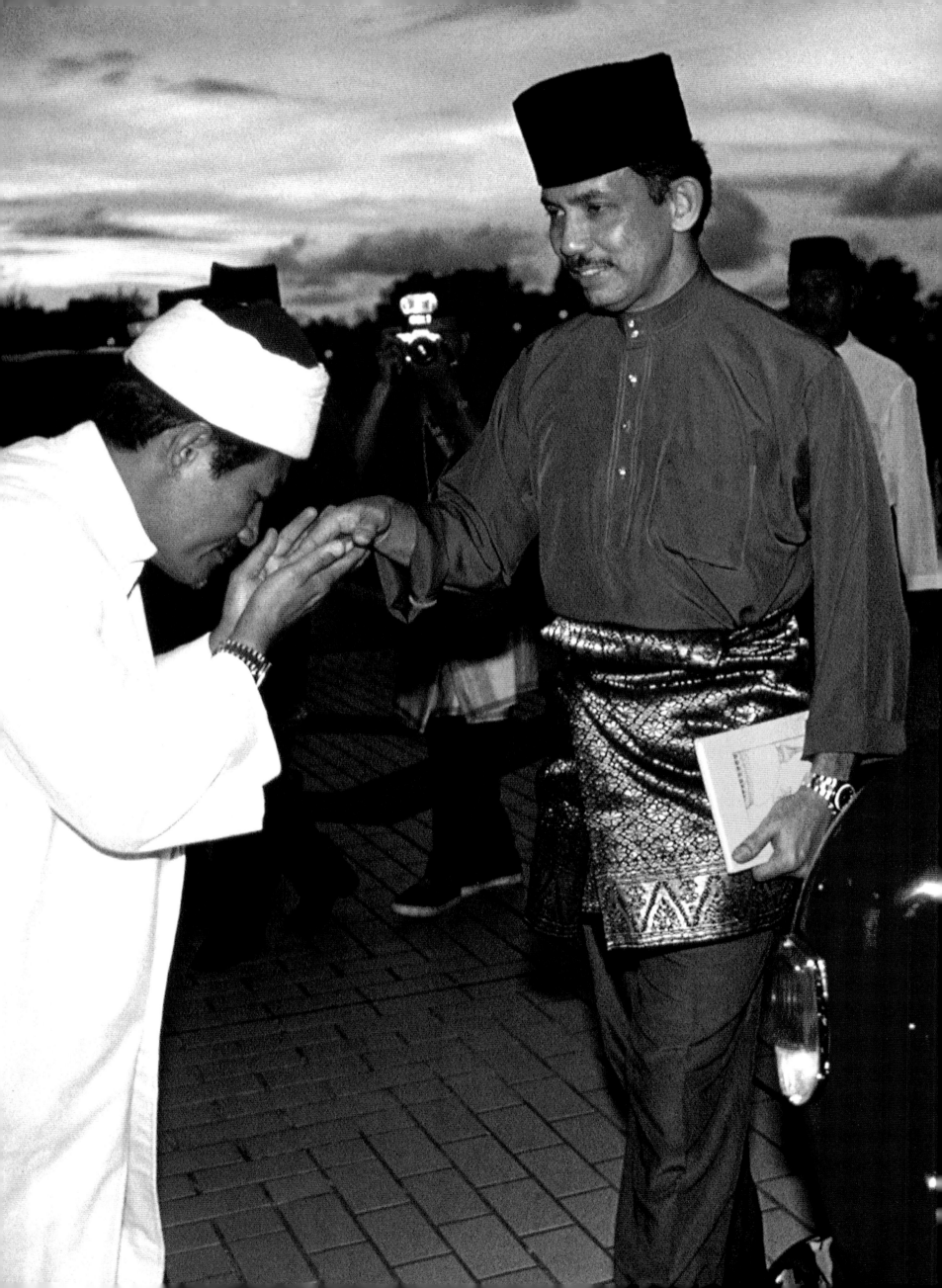

Mohd Yusof Mohd Yassin

Sultan Haji Hassanal Bolkiah of Brunei Darussalam arrives for evening prayers at the Omar Ali Saifuddien Mosque (preceding pages). During his frequent public appearances, he meets and talks to as many of his subjects as possible to learn more about their wellbeing (above and right).

Mohd Yusof Mohd Yassin

Gueorgui Pinkhassov

Tara Sosrowardoyo

Lim Bee Ngo

S ultan Haji Hassanal Bolkiah
celebrated the 25th year of his accession to the throne of Brunei
Darussalam with one of the most vivid royal celebrations in
South-east Asia. The highlight was the procession through the
streets of the capital, the sparkling gold and black chariot
carrying the Sultan glittering in the sunshine (preceding pages
and top right). Preceding pages also show court officials bearing
ceremonial shields in a tradition laden with symbolism,
while the cheering, flag-bearing crowds (above and right
bottom) are at once an affirmation of the Sultan's
special position and of the longevity of tradition.

Hj Kamaluddin PDP Hj Abu Bakar

Hj Kamaluddin PDP Hj Abu Bakar

Tara Sosrowardoyo

D espite its modern architecture, the Istana Nurul Iman, official residence and workplace of the Sultan of Brunei Darussalam, remains true to its Malay roots, as can be seen both in its interiors and in the roles of Palace officials. The entrance to the Throne Room is guarded by the *Panglima Raja* (above), who bears the musket or *pemuras* and bullet case (*kampil peluru*), and the *Panglima Asgar* (right), who bears a shield and sword of traditional design. These officers, with their ancient titles, have a ceremonial function, while other security officers in modern uniform have a new role to play.

Hj Kamaluddin PDP Hj Abu Bakar

Tara Sosrowardoyo

Brunei Darussalam's commitment to upholding its centuries-old royal heritage is given expression in the Royal Regalia Building or *Bangunan Alat Kebesaran Di Raja*. Here, the unique and colourful royal regalia are seen on public display, from the magnificent *perisai kerajaan* or royal shields (preceding right), carried by the sons of *cheteria* during state ceremonies, to an array of royal umbrellas, including the *payung dadu*, eight multi-coloured umbrellas, and the *payung kawan*, 40 umbrellas in yellow and red check (preceding left). Tradition is also present in the Islamic arches dominating the Throne Room (above), where regalia-bearing officials stand on duty during the Sultan's birthday investiture of honours.

Tara Sosrowardoyo

Seated in the main body of the Throne Room, an expectant audience awaits the arrival of the Sultan to take his place beneath the royal canopy for the conferring of titles on his birthday. The Throne Room, with its massive crystal chandeliers, reflects the age-old dignity and majesty of the ancient royal court of Brunei Darussalam.

Tara Sosrowardoyo

S ultan Haji Hassanal Bolkiah
in the Throne Room with the Raja Isteri, Pengiran Isteri and
court officials (above), during his birthday investiture ceremony.
Apart from the Palace, other major formal events take place in
the *Lapau* or Royal Ceremonial Hall, where the Sultan was
crowned in 1968, and where he is shown seated beneath a
splendid golden canopy (left). The magnificent interiors of
the Istana Nurul Iman are a fitting setting for the formal
banquet for Heads of State, part of the celebrations
during the Sultan's Silver Jubilee year (preceding pages).

Tara Sosrowardoyo

The brothers and sons of the Sultan hold traditional titles in the ancient court hierarchy, and two of his brothers also serve in the Government. The picture above shows, from left, Prince Sufri, Prince Al-Muhtadee Billah, Prince Mohamed and Prince Jefri. Picture (top right) shows Prince Al-Muhtadee Billah in the school library, and (bottom right) the Sultan with his sons, Prince Al-Muhtadee Billah and Prince Azim.

Sulaiman Hj Mahmud

Abbas

Tara Sosrowardoyo

T he mace-bearer leads the
Sultan past groups of graduating students on Convocation Day at
the Universiti Brunei Darussalam. The university was founded by
the Sultan in 1985 with the aim of producing a qualified
Bruneian workforce, while at the same time abiding by the
tenets of Islam in the form of teaching. To this end, the
western-style mace seen here has recently been superceded
as a symbol of authority by a special hand-written Qu'ran,
the *Mushaf Universiti Brunei Darussalam*.

Tara Sosrowardoyo

An informal moment
during a portrait session at the Universiti Brunei Darussalam
shows the Sultan dressed in his robes of office as Chancellor.
With him is his daughter, Yang Teramat Mulia Paduka Seri
Pengiran Anak Puteri Hajah Rashidah, a new graduate
of the university.

5

TODAY'S PROSPERITY TOMORROW'S PROMISE

Gerald Gay

U ltimately, a country's strength and hope for the future resides in the younger generation, and Brunei Darussalam has a predominantly young population, half of which is under the age of twenty. This situation represents both a challenge and a promise — whether in the friendly smile of this young girl traditionally dressed in her *tudong* (above), or in the baffled look of a youngster kitted out in the latest stone-washed denim (right). The modern aspect of the country is shown in an aerial panorama (preceding pages).

Wang Miao

Mike Yamashita

The smiling face of this girl seems acknowledgment enough that the Government of Brunei Darussalam has given high priority to the provision of education. There are now about 190 schools, ranging from pre-primary to tertiary, throughout the country, and the educational network supports full and free tuition for citizens up to university standard.

Raghu Rai

B y educating its children, Brunei Darussalam assures itself of a highly trained workforce in years to come. This boy knows that his future is in good hands as national spending on education attests, with more than B$380 million budgeted for building of schools for the five-year period 1991-1995. Vocational and technical training are available in the country as well, including an agricultural training college at Sinaut.

Mohd Yusof Mohd Yassin

A ttentive pupils in this Kuala Belait school are under the charge of 1992 Teacher of the Year, Hajah Rashidah binti OKP Abdul Rashid (top right), while a daily routine familiar to all Bruneians ensures personal hygiene in the classroom (bottom right). A teacher at the Maktab Duli Pengiran Muda Al-Muhtadee Billah Pre-university College supervises a laboratory lesson (above). Most secondary schools offer modern science as part of the school syllabus.

Ara Guler

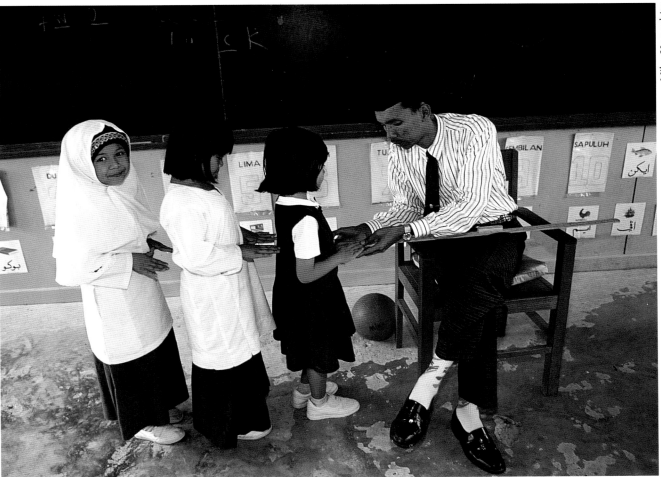

Mike Yamashita

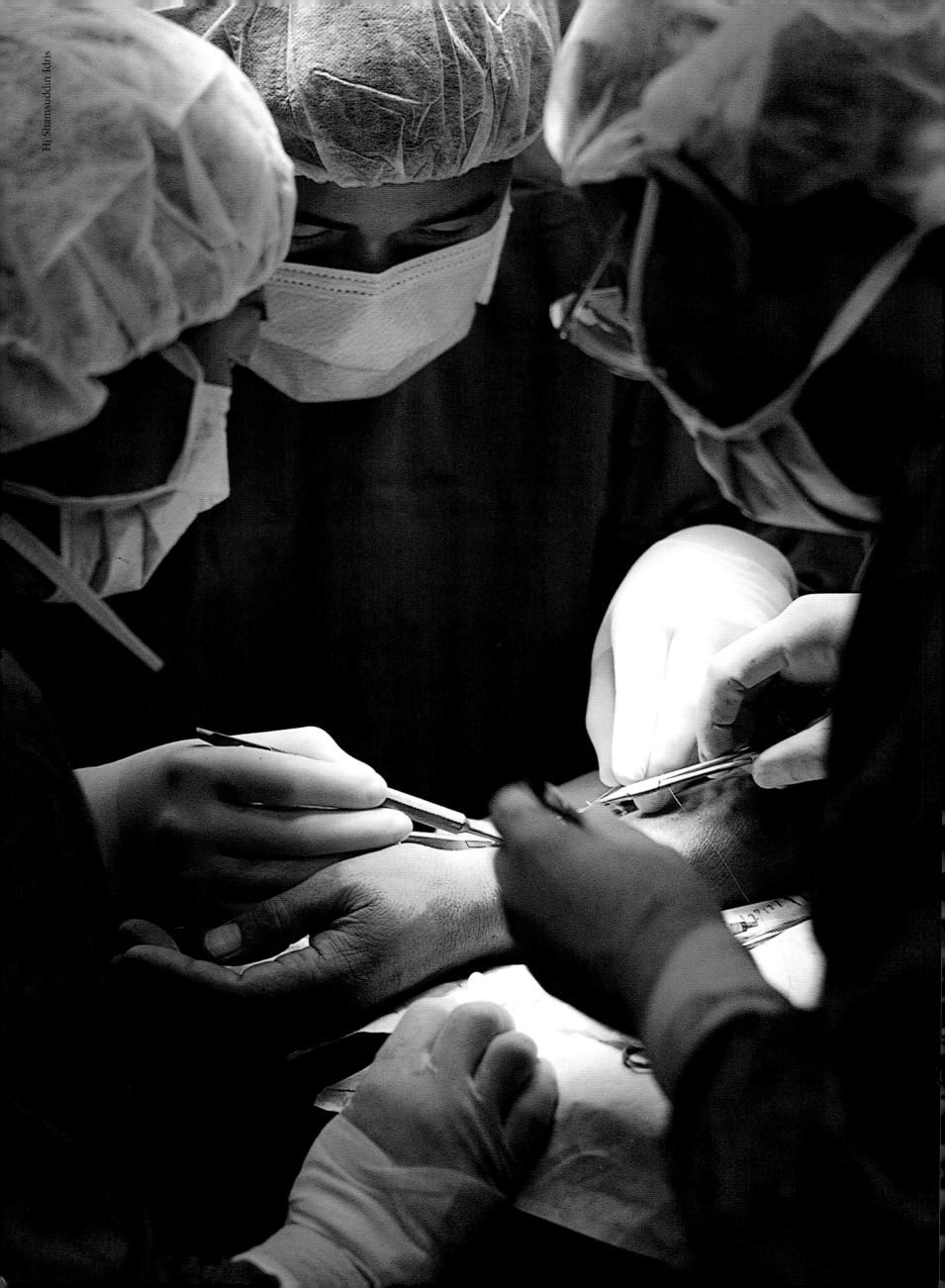

Tara Sostrowardoyo

Brunei Darussalam boasts a standard of healthcare and life expectancy fully comparable to the highest international standards. Healthcare is available to all, from an emergency arm operation using the most sophisticated equipment in the capital's RIPAS Hospital (left), to a helicopter-borne flying doctor service that takes regular and prompt medical treatment to remote areas (above).

151

Leong Ka Tai

B runei's national defence force, first established as the Brunei Malay Regiment, became the Royal Brunei Armed Forces in 1983, and here the Commander of the Royal Brunei Armed Forces (left), is seen decorating a newly-promoted officer, while a parade ground scene demonstrates the dexterity of drill sergeants (above). The rigours of parading in the heat of the tropical sun are vividly evoked overleaf.

Leong Ka Tai

Tara Sosrowardoyo

Brunei Darussalam's armed forces comprise land, naval and air units, grouped together as a brigade spearheaded by two infantry battalions. Based at Muara deep-sea port (above and right) is a flotilla of fast coastal and patrol vessels armed with surface-to-surface missiles, one of the many high-tech systems the country has provided for its security.

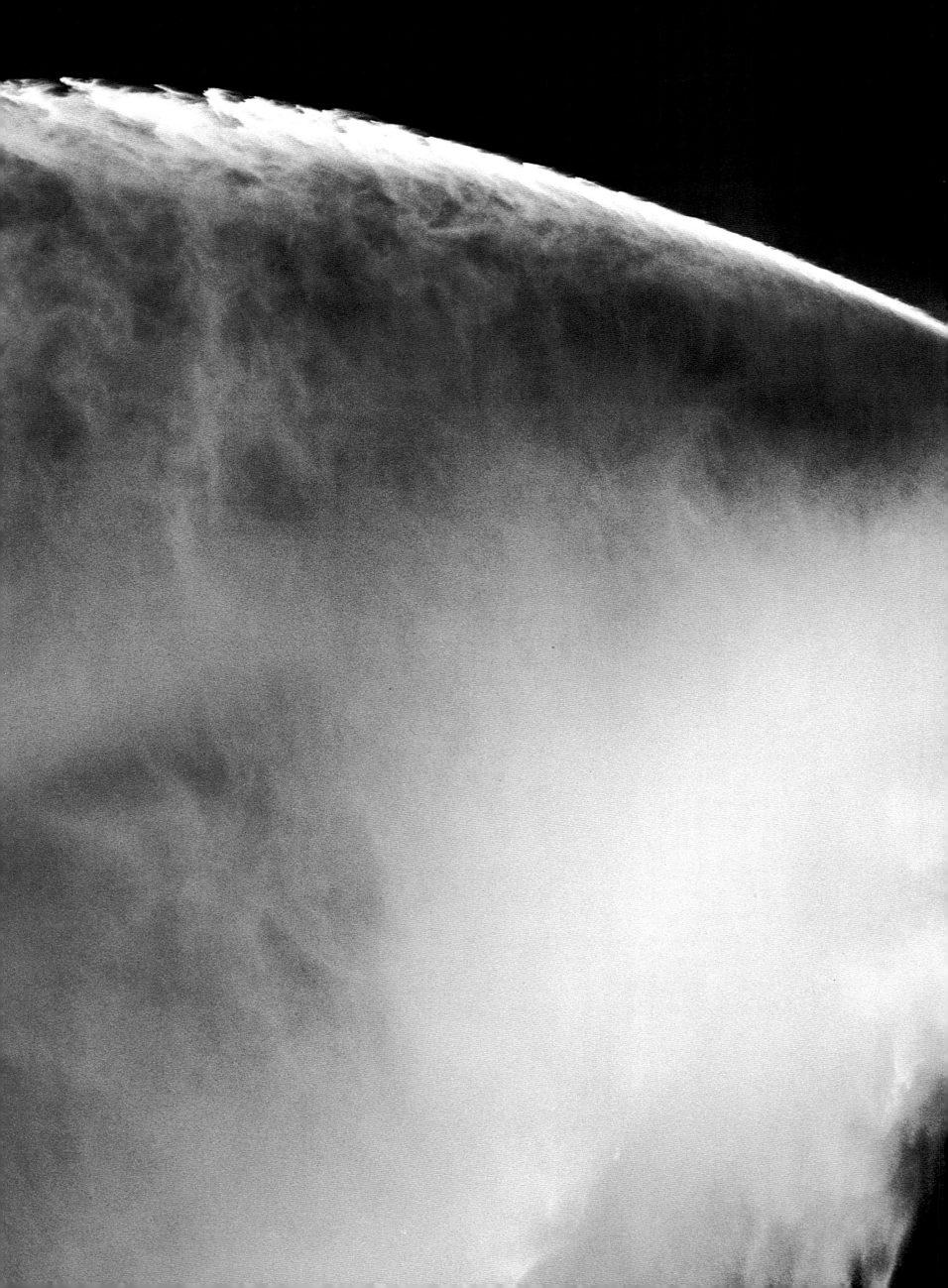

Gueorgui Pinkhassov

A dramatic crescent of water erupts from the diving vessel docking ship, which doubles as a fire-fighting vessel for offshore operations (preceding pages). Oil, and in the last two decades gas, have mainly been extracted offshore, and the largest of the offshore structures, the Champion 7 Complex, covers an area large enough to accommodate 200 people. Among the facilities servicing the complex is a helicopter shuttle which ferries about 360,000 people for offshore operations a year (above). Picture (left) shows a worker on board a liquefied natural gas (LNG) tanker, used to transport the LNG to Japan.

Dominic Sansoni

Peter Chen

Rio Helmi
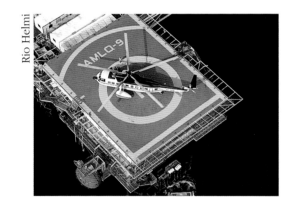

Tara Sosrowardoyo

THE MODERN FACE OF BRUNEI DARUSSALAM IS MOST PROMINENTLY SEEN IN THE OIL AND GAS INDUSTRY, WHERE STATE-OF-THE-ART EQUIPMENT AND A COMPLEX NETWORK OF OFFSHORE FACILITIES HELP EXPLOIT THE SUBTERRANEAN WEALTH BELOW THE SOUTH CHINA SEA THAT HAS GIVEN THE NATION ONE OF THE HIGHEST LIVING STANDARDS IN THE WORLD TODAY.

Abbas

Dominic Sansoni

Dominic Sansoni

Peter Chen

Rio Helmi

Abbas

FROM THE DRILLING FLOOR OF AN OFFSHORE RIG TO THE HI-TECH PRECISION OF A SATELLITE POSITIONING SYSTEM, AN INTRICATE AND COMPLEX INTERPLAY OF TASKS AND SKILLS ENSURES THE EFFICIENT AND SAFE EXTRACTION OF OIL AND GAS, THE PRECIOUS SUBSTANCES THAT FUEL THE ENGINE OF MODERN BRUNEIAN COMMERCE AND INDUSTRY.

Dominic Sansoni

Peter Chen

Hj Yacob Dato Paduka Hj Sunny

Great importance is laid on health, safety and environment policies throughout Brunei Shell's operation, from the provision of correct protective clothing to comprehensive facilities for combatting major incidents. Equipment and personnel are on 24-hour standby at all times (right), and Brunei Shell's own fire service is maintained in a state of constant readiness, as this training exercise at the Brunei Liquefied Natural Gas (BLNG) Plant at Lumut testifies (above).

Peter Chen

T he BLNG plant was the first large-scale plant of its kind in the world when it went onstream in 1972. Twenty years later, it was again the focus of industry attention when it became the first LNG plant to undergo a major rejuvenation programme designed to carry it though another 20 years of operations. It annually exports more than five million tonnes of LNG to customers in Japan.

Peter Chen

T he BLNG plant is shown here
dramatically silhouetted against a glowing flare. Natural gas
becomes liquid at -157 degrees centigrade, at which temperature
it occupies just one six-hundredth of its space as a gas, stored
in heavily-insulated, double-skinned tanks. The off-boil
from the evaporating gas is used to turn the ship's
turbines during the six-day journey to Japan.

167

Dominic Sansoni

Tommy Chang

Tommy Chang

Offshore oil operations
continue 24 hours a day, from the loading of an oil tanker via a
single buoy mooring (top left) linked by undersea pipeline to
the coast, to diving operations (above). Divers breathe
an oxygen-helium mix as they work in depths of
up to 60 metres, using a diving bell (bottom left)
as their base for each eight-hour shift.

Emil Davocol

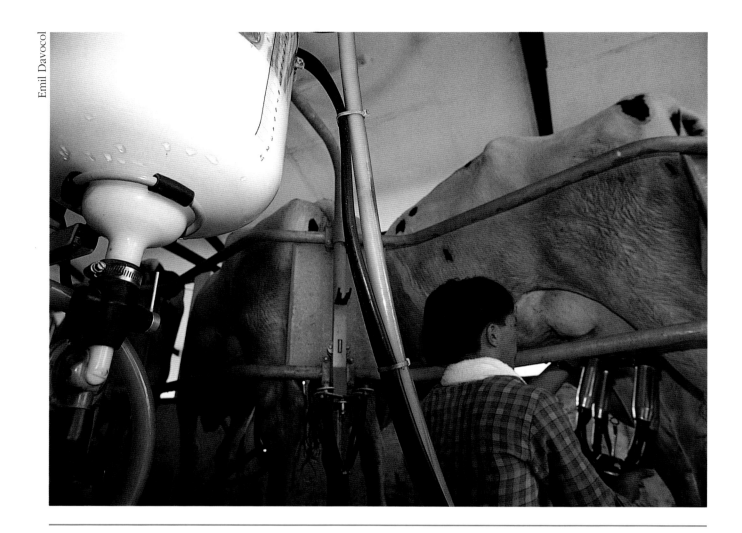

S elf-sufficiency is an important
goal for Brunei Darussalam, and intensive research and training
have been directed to this end. Two key concerns are rice and
beef, and much of Brunei Darussalam's beef requirements
are met by ownership of three large cattle stations in
Australia's Northern Territory. Another agricultural
project is the Brunei Dairy Farm at Jerudong.

Emil Davocol

H ere a packing machine operator loads a van for distributing the finished milk product. A number of other research programmes have also been launched, leading to success in egg production, vegetable and fruit farming and fisheries. Diversification is perhaps the Government's most important development goal.

Emil Davocol

S uccessive National Development
Plans have emphasised self-reliance and the creation of a secure
base of local light industry, both to diversify the industrial base
and to reduce reliance on imported goods and expertise. Success
in this field is demonstrated by the finished products rolling off
the production line at the Interline Roofing Company
(left) and the successful production and marketing
of Sehat, Brunei Darussalam's own purified
water (above).

Leong Ka Tai

A futuristic decoration hanging beside the Brunei River in Bandar Seri Begawan during the Silver Jubilee celebrations (above) echoes the form of a Royal Brunei jet, undergoing servicing (right top). Royal Brunei Airlines (RBA) was founded in 1974, and has a modern fleet of Boeings, including five wide-bodied B767-300 extended range aircraft, that fly regularly between Europe, the Middle and Far East, South-east Asia and Australia. It recruits cabin crew from all the ASEAN nations, and is famous for its first-class cabins and the quality of its staff, all of whom undergo intensive training. These cabin crew (bottom right), have just graduated.

Picture courtesy of RBA

Raghu Rai

Rio Helmi

Bandar Seri Begawan's new Islamic Bank of Brunei building, pictured with its architect, Haji Idris bin Abas (right), is one of the capital's new landmarks. It puts high-tech architecture to the service of Islamic business practice. Several succeeding National Development Plans have highlighted the need for new housing for resettlement purposes, and this aerial view (above) of Berakas shows one of many such schemes. Following pages show a blend of old and new as a solitary figure wearing the traditional *tudong* walks towards the capital's modern skyline.

Tara Sosrowardoyo

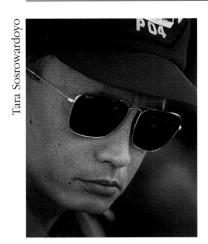

Peter Chen

Gerald Gay

Dominic Sansoni

AN IMPRESSIONISTIC PATCHWORK OF PORTRAITS CAPTURES THE VITALITY AND CULTURAL VARIETY THAT IS THE TRUE STRENGTH OF BRUNEI DARUSSALAM, FROM THE PURPOSEFUL PROFILE OF A PATROL BOAT COMMANDER IN THE COUNTRY'S DEFENCE FORCE AND THE CHEERFUL SMILE OF A YOUNGSTER, TO THE SERENE FACE OF A MOTHER.

Dominic Sansoni

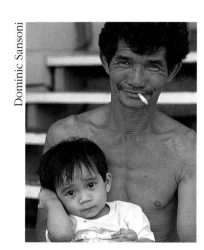

Hj Yacob Dato Paduka Hj Sunny

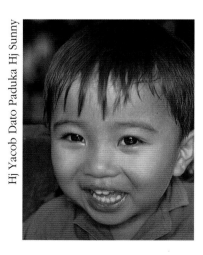

Tommy Chang

Dennis Lau

Leong Ka Tai

Ara Guler

CANDID IMAGES ENCAPSULATE THE MODERN HEART OF THE BRUNEIAN NATION, FROM THE GLANCE OF A YOUNG GIRL IN A BECOMING RED *TUDONG,* AND THE EXPERIENCED LOOK OF A *KAPITAN CHINA* (CHINESE COMMUNITY LEADER) TO THE WEATHERED FACE OF A FISHERMAN AND THE GRACEFUL POSTURE OF A TRADITIONAL BRUNEIAN DANCER.

Hiroshi Suga

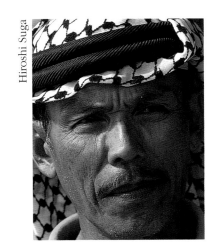

Gerald Gay

Leong Ka Tai

Brunei Darussalam is home to a
wealth of creative talent, and many art, photography and
handicraft exhibitions are staged regularly in the country (left).
Artist Pengiran Dato Paduka Hj Asmalee bin Pengiran
Ahmad, Director of Youth and Sports, is seen at work on
a portrait of the Sultan's daughter, Yang Teramat
Mulia Paduka Seri Pengiran Anak Puteri Hajah
Rashidah (above).

Tara Sosrowardoyo

Hj Kamaluddin PDP Hj Abu Bakar

Tara Sosrowardoyo

P hysical sports and recreation
are becoming increasingly popular among the youth of Brunei
Darussalam, with skateboarding and swimming (left) attracting
particular enthusiasm. These modern sports co-exist with ancient
Malay pastimes such as the martial art *silat*, the rattan ball game
sepak takraw and top-spinning (*gasing*), which still retain their
following. Brunei Darussalam's modern sports facilities are
second-to-none, as this study of a weight-lifter (above)
in the 35,000-seat Hassanal Bolkiah National
Stadium shows.

185

Gerald Gay

I s there a modern Brunei trend?
The evidence of these young Bruneians would argue that there
is, and that it encompasses a strong sense of colour and
traditional costumes. The young man (above) takes a break from
a wedding celebration. His white *songkok* probably indicates that
he has performed the *haj* at a relatively young age. This
student in school uniform (right) sports a new mountain
bike. Young Bruneians keep up to date with the
latest trends in sports and leisure activities.

Gerald Gay

Hiroshi Suga

Hiroshi Suga

As dusk falls and the heat of the day fades, the night air is filled with the sights, sounds and smells of the foodstalls which spring to life in the Tamu Kianggeh market and in the car park near the Omar Ali Saifuddien Mosque. There is a wide range of Malay, Indonesian, Chinese and Indian dishes. Fresh fish, from the bountiful waters of Brunei Bay and a staple food of the Bruneian diet, are particularly evident, and are shown here being grilled to a tantalising crispness (above and left bottom).

Hj Shamsuddin Idris

Brunei Darussalam now has
one of the most up-to-date television networks in South-east
Asia. The technically sophisticated and state-run Radio Television
Brunei (right) broadcasts a wide variety of entertainment
and drama programmes, a growing proportion of
which are produced locally, such as the traditional
Malay variety programme shown above.

Hj Kamaluddin PDP Hj Abu Bakar

Duangdao Suwanarungsi

Tara Sosrowardoyo

The mood mellows at dusk in
the capital, where one brightly-lit landmark is the Royal Regalia
Building (left bottom). It was built for the Sultan's Silver Jubilee,
a tumultuous celebration that continued for more than
a month, featuring a colourful procession of floats
on the Brunei River (left top) and a dazzling
fireworks display (overleaf).

Tara Sosrowardoyo

Tara Sosrowardoyo

The traditional Malay architecture of the Istana Nurul Iman, with its long sloping roofs, is reflected in the peaceful waters of the Brunei River. The Istana, the world's largest residential Palace which also houses the Prime Minister's Office and the Ministry of Defence, was completed in 1983 as Brunei Darussalam prepared to take its place in the world community as a fully independent nation.

APPENDIXES

DIARY OF THE PROJECT
198

MAP OF BRUNEI DARUSSALAM
PHOTOGRAPHERS' BIOGRAPHIES
200

GROUP PHOTOGRAPH
202

TABLE OF MOTIFS
204

INDEX
206

BIBLIOGRAPHY
207

ACKNOWLEDGEMENTS
208

Octover 24, 1992, Bandar Seri Begawan: An air of nervous excitement bathes the nerve centre on the second floor of the Sheraton Utama Hotel. In one corner, three photographers huddle over a map of Brunei Darussalam while Peter Schoppert, Project Editor, and Tara Sosrowardoyo, Chief Photographer, quietly brief Thai photographer S. Duangdao on her rainforest assignment. Project Manager Shamira Bhanu takes yet another phone call, this time from the Ministry of Industry and Primary Resources, raising her voice to be heard over the hubbub of welcome for the latest batch of overseas photographers to arrive. It is 12 hours before the dawn of the week-long photo shoot and there is still much to be done – faxes to be sent, phone calls to be made, photographers to be briefed and transport chased up. After seven months' of intense preparation, it was difficult to believe that the event was so close.

The buildup really began in April 1992 in more relaxed circumstances when Brunei Shell appointed Editions Didier Millet, a Singapore-based publishing house, to produce a major photographic book on Brunei Darussalam to coincide with the 25th anniversary of His Majesty Sultan Haji Hassanal Bolkiah's accession to the throne. The idea of 25 world-acclaimed photographers capturing the country on film, against the backdrop of one of the most vivid royal celebrations seen in South-east Asia, was an exciting proposition, and all 25 photographers, including four Bruneians, instantly accepted the invitation.

Both EDM and Brunei Shell had agreed that the shoot would take place between October 25 and 31, 1992. That left little time for the numerous jobs that needed to be done before the photographers descended on the country. Flights were arranged, re-arranged and altered again, visas and press passes applied for, customs clearance obtained for photographic equipment, some 1,750 rolls of professional film ordered, and transport and accommodation booked.

Everyone knew from the start that this was no ordinary project, and Brunei Shell often emphasised the need to capture the country's unique qualities, including its subtle blend of modernity and tradition, rich Islamic heritage and the continuity that comes from one of the longest unbroken royal lines in the world. The project team spent a considerable time in Brunei Darussalam, acquiring a feel for the country and its people and researching assignment lists so that the photographers could come to grips fast with their assignments. It meant a whirlwind rush of meetings with key people, including officials in ministries and district offices. Too many to mention, they include Haji Hazair bin Hj Abdullah, Director of Information, who helped develop assignments; Pehin Jamil, Head of the History Centre, who gave invaluable background on Brunei Darussalam's rich past; and Awang Rushdie bin Hj Abd Latif, of the Ministry of Defence, who arranged access to military activities.

Haji Kamaluddin PDP Haji Abu Bakar, President of the Brunei Photographic Society and one of the 25 photographers, was invaluable as the project's Local Representative, as he knew practically everyone and time and again succeeded in getting access to people whose expertise could be tapped for the job. Brunei Shell's Public Affairs Adviser Hussin bin Ahmad worked hard as well, networking with the different sectors of the community to establish a representative concept for the book. The project's profile was further raised by

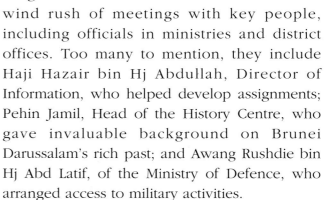

PROJECT ADVISER PRINCE HAJI SUFRI BOLKIAH HOSTS A WELCOME PARTY FOR THE PHOTOGRAPHERS AT THE SHERATON POOLSIDE ON THE EVE OF THE SHOOT. HE TOOK THE FIRST PICTURE OF THE PROJECT, A PORTRAIT OF PROJECT MEMBERS AND PHOTOGRAPHERS (BELOW). WITH THE PRINCE (ABOVE) IS RON VAN DEN BERG, MANAGING DIRECTOR OF BRUNEI SHELL PETROLEUM, WHICH FINANCED AND CO-ORDINATED THE PROJECT.

two nationwide photography competitions, the biggest-ever to be staged in the country and timed to coincide with the photo shoot.

It was crucial to find co-ordinators who could help with the assignments and accompany the photographers as guides and interpreters. Haji Kamaluddin proposed using the services of members of the Brunei Photographic Society, all talented amateurs and many of them senior officers in the Government. Forty members were speedily enlisted as Host Photographic Co-ordinators and set to work on logistical mat-

ters, like arranging transport and accommodation to outlying areas, and ensuring that permission was granted for photography.

The nerve centre for the project was the Sheraton Utama, which supplied 50 rooms free of charge and put up the photographers at a special rate. Teams were set up to brief the photographers, and each given 70 rolls of film. On the eve of the shoot, Prince Haji Sufri Bolkiah, Project Adviser, hosted a welcome party for the photographers at the hotel poolside. In a speech, Mr Ron van den Berg, Brunei Shell Petroleum's Managing Director, thanked His Majesty the Sultan for consenting to write a foreword and welcomed photographers to the project, which he described as one of the most ambitious of its kind seen in Brunei Darussalam. "Look at the country with a fresh eye and use your long experience and critical expertise to capture the heart of the nation," he told them.

While some made Bandar Seri Begawan their base for the entire week, a number stayed in Kuala Belait and two in Temburong, covering the lifestyles of people living in the interior and the work of Brunei Shell on the coast and offshore. After a hard day's work, the Bandar Seri Begawan-based photographers usually gathered in the operations centre to swap stories over cups of coffee. There were many incidents to relate, some amusing and others simply hilarious. Such as the one involving Russian photographer Pinkhassov, who unwittingly availed himself of the open-handed generosity

of Bruneians. It happened when he and his companion were drawn by the sound of loud music into what they took to be a restaurant in Kampong Ayer. They were welcomed, ate some food and spent a relaxing hour chatting. It was only when the owner refused to bring a bill that it began to dawn that they were being entertained in a private home.

Wildlife photographer Slim Sreedharan of Malaysia, banished to the jungles in pursuit of the elusive proboscis monkey, discovered he had an unsuspected talent for writing. His roll-notes showed a lyrical style, describing encounters with smiling redshanks and almost-smiling snakes, as well as the difficulties he experienced in trying to take pictures while, as he put it, "levitating with metronomic precision" on a speedboat travelling too fast for comfort.

As for Dominic Sansoni, of Sri Lanka, and Peter Chen, of Singapore — sent to photograph Brunei Shell — so reluctant were they to leave their assignments that they almost missed the farewell dinner hosted by Prince Haji Sufri Bolkiah to mark the end of the shoot.

Bruneian photographer Haji Shamsuddin Idris needed a strong stomach to take pictures in an operating theatre of the Suri Seri Begawan Hospital, while Bruneian photographic co-ordinator Jeaniffah binte Hj Md Yusof entered a man's world, with a gruelling schedule that included several nights on offshore oil platforms. Bruneian host co-ordinator Haji Hamdi bin OKSR Hj Md Nor summed up the shoot thus: "It was hard work but a great experience, and I think we all learned from each other."

On the last day, photographers and project members lingered in the Sheraton Utama lobby, exchanging addresses, reluctant to say goodbye. For the photographers, it marked the end of the shoot, but for the project team, it was the start of the next challenging phase — developing the rolls of film, selecting and photo-editing from 70,000-odd pictures, and putting together a book that would do justice to Brunei Darussalam — Abode of Peace.

PRINCE SUFRI (LEFT) AT THE GROUP PHOTOGRAPHY SESSION HELD AT SUNGEI KEDAYAN TO MARK THE END OF THE SHOOT. THESE CHILDREN (BELOW) ARE AMONG THE MANY PARTICIPANTS AT THE CHILDREN'S PHOTOGRAPHY COMPETITION AT ANDUKI LAKE, ONE OF TWO NATIONWIDE COMPETITIONS ORGANISED BY BRUNEI SHELL TO COINCIDE WITH THE SHOOT.

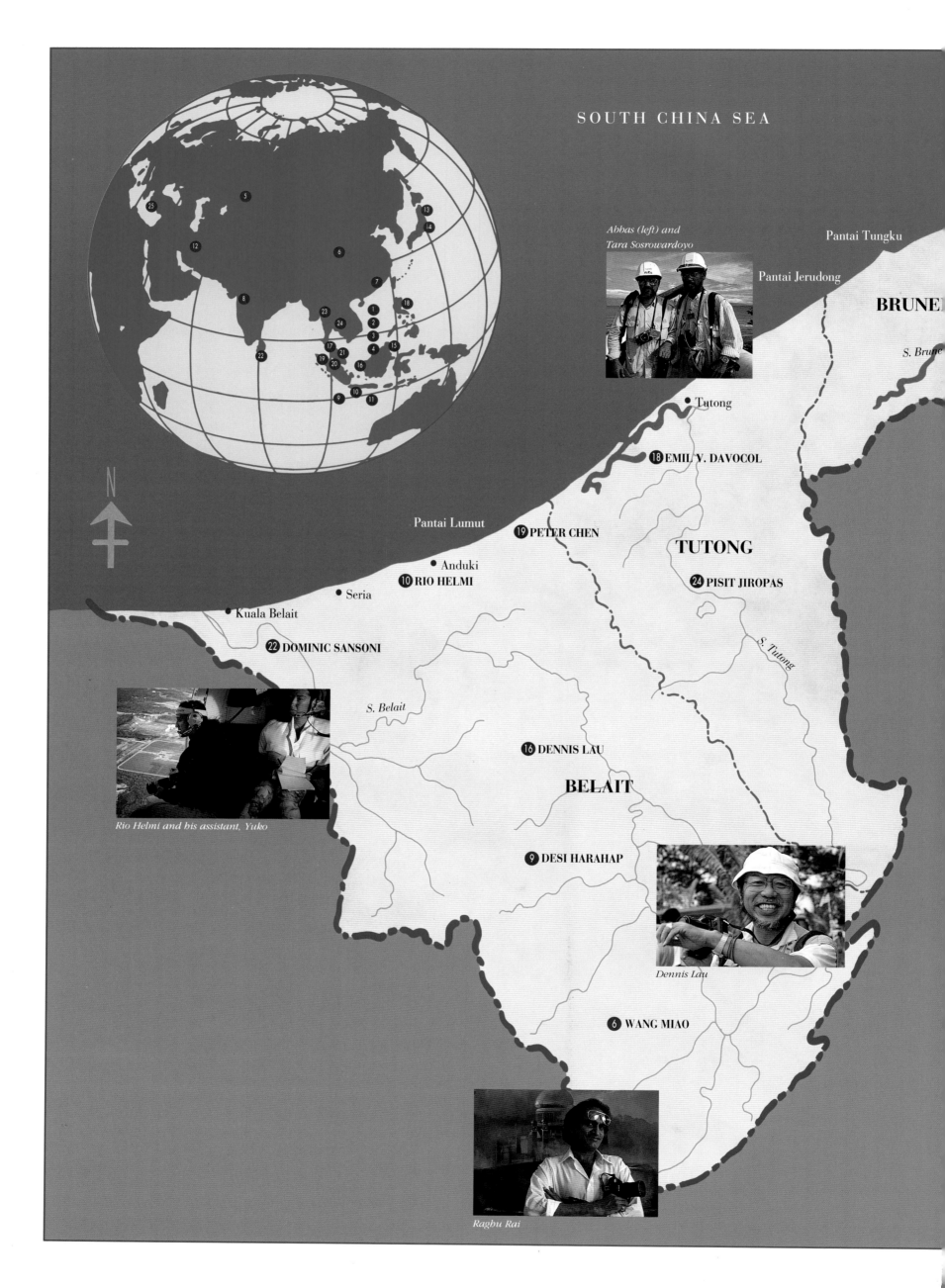

SOUTH CHINA SEA

*Abbas (left) and
Tara Sosrowardoyo*

Pantai Tungku

Pantai Jerudong

BRUNEI

S. Brunei

• Tutong

18 EMIL V. DAVOCOL

Pantai Lumut

19 PETER CHEN

TUTONG

S. Tutong

• Anduki

24 PISIT JIROPAS

10 RIO HELMI

• Seria

• Kuala Belait

22 DOMINIC SANSONI

S. Belait

Rio Helmi and his assistant, Yuko

16 DENNIS LAU

BELAIT

9 DESI HARAHAP

Dennis Lau

6 WANG MIAO

Raghu Rai

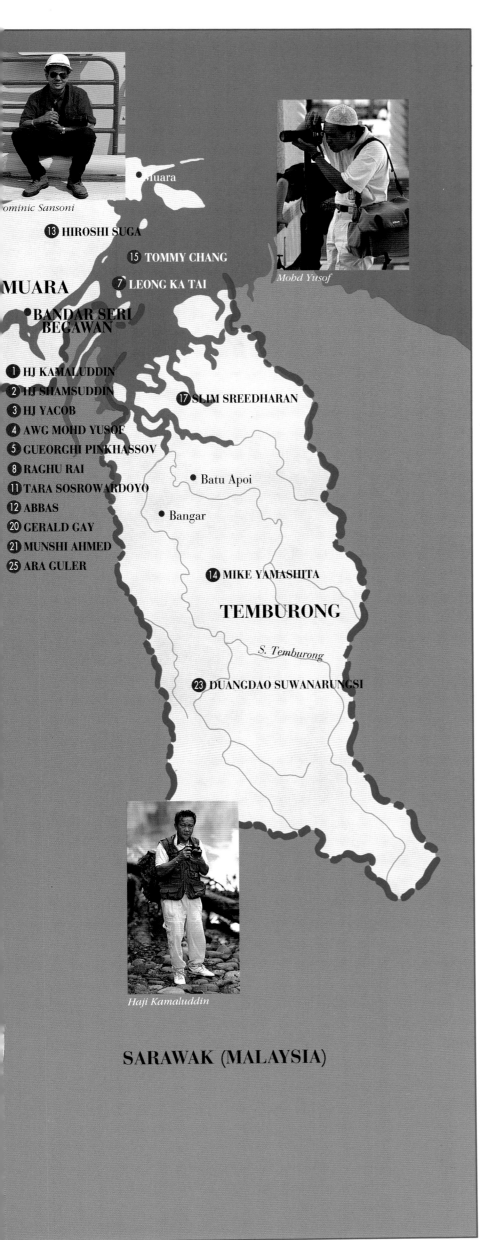

Dominic Sansoni

⑬ HIROSHI SUGA

⑮ TOMMY CHANG

⑦ LEONG KA TAI

Mohd Yusof

MUARA

• BANDAR SERI BEGAWAN

① HJ KAMALUDDIN
② HJ SHAMSUDDIN
③ HJ YACOB
④ AWG MOHD YUSOF
⑤ GUEORGHI PINKHASSOV
⑧ RAGHU RAI
⑪ TARA SOSROWARDOYO
⑫ ABBAS
⑳ GERALD GAY
㉑ MUNSHI AHMED
㉕ ARA GULER

⑰ SLIM SREEDHARAN

• Batu Apoi

• Bangar

⑭ MIKE YAMASHITA

TEMBURONG

S. Temburong

㉓ DUANGDAO SUWANARUNGSI

Haji Kamaluddin

SARAWAK (MALAYSIA)

PHOTOGRAPHERS' BIOGRAPHIES

① HJ KAMALUDDIN PDP HJ ABU BAKAR (*Brunei Darussalam*)
Hj Kamaluddin is the President of the Brunei Photographic Society and one of Brunei Darussalam's foremost photographers. An ardent photo enthusiast since his youth, he was appointed Host Photographer for the book project.

② HJ SHAMSUDDIN IDRIS (*Brunei Darussalam*)
A talented award-winning photographer and member of the A.R.P.S., Hj Shamsuddin is also well-known in Brunei Darussalam for his singing and acting abilities. He is currently working with Radio Television Brunei (RTB).

③ HJ YACOB DATO PADUKA HJ SUNNY (*Brunei Darussalam*)
A gifted photographer in his spare time, Hj Yacob is Head of Film/ English Services, RTB. He has been the recipient of many local and international awards and is a member of the A.R.P.S.

④ MOHD YUSOF MOHD YASSIN (*Brunei Darussalam*)
Hon. Secretary of the Brunei Photographic Society, Mohd Yusof works as TV Vision Supervisor at RTB. Among the photographic awards he has won is a merit award at the Islamic Photographic Competition in Turkey.

⑤ GUEORGHI PINKHASSOV (*Central Asia*)
Moscow-born Pinkhassov is an independent photojournalist for a number of magazines, among them *Time* and *Newsweek*. He lives in Paris, and is a member of the Magnum Photo Agency.

⑥ WANG MIAO (*China*)
A photographer for *China Tourism* magazine in Hong Kong, Wang's evocative photo study, *Poems Collected from the Open Country*, was published in 1982 by *China Photography* magazine. She was a principal contributor to the commemorative photo album, *Grief of the People*, which conveys the depth of sorrow following the death of Premier Zhou Enlai in 1976.

⑦ LEONG KA TAI (*Hong Kong*)
Leong focuses mainly on editorial and corporate photography. His pictures have been published in international magazines, including *Stern*, and various books, including *China: The Long March*, *Salute to Singapore*, *Beijing* and *The Taste of China*.

⑧ RAGHU RAI (*India*)
A photographer since 1966, Rai is a contributor to *Time*, *National Geographic* and *Paris Match*. He was invited to join Magnum Photo Agency in 1976. Widely exhibited, he has 25' of his photographs in the permanent collection of the Bibliotheque Nationale in Paris, and has published *Delhi: A Portrait of Indhira Gandhi*, *The Taj Mahal*, *Calcutta*, *Khajuraho*, and *Forever in Bloom*.

⑨ DESI HARAHAP (*Indonesia*)
Harahap attended the Cinematography Academy in Jakarta (IKAJ) and has worked in feature film-making. She has since moved on to more journalistic work, reporting on remote regions of Indonesia. She currently works as photo-editor of the weekly magazine *Jakarta-Jakarta*.

⑩ RIO HELMI (*Indonesia*)
Bali-based Helmi has worked for 10 years in the Indonesian media, as editor of the *Sunday Bali Post* and associate editor of *Mutiara* magazine. He has also worked on film production and press promotions. He is a partner in Image Network Indonesia.

⑪ TARA SOSROWARDOYO (*Indonesia*)
New York-born Sosrowardoyo, Chief Photographer for the project, now lives in Jakarta. A psychology and graphic design major, he made photography — which he studied as a minor — his career. He produces audio-visual programmes for industry and tourism, and works on commercial and editorial assignments. He helped form the Zoom Photographic Agency in 1980.

⑫ ABBAS (*Iran*)
A member of the Magnum Photo Agency, he has covered, since 1970, major political events in Africa, the Middle East, Latin America and Europe. An Iranian and a Muslim, he has a particularly strong interest in Islamic subjects.

⑬ HIROSHI SUGA (*Japan*)
Winner of the 1987 Ken Domon Award. Suga's various books on Bali, including *Bali Entranced* and *Bali: The Demonic, the Godly and the Wondrous*, have received international acclaim. He has also held one-man shows in Japan and the United States.

⑭ MIKE YAMASHITA (*Japan*)
Yamashita is a regular contributor to *National Geographic* and *Time* and travels all over the world for Nikon, Singapore Airlines and Diners Club. His book, *Lakes, Peaks and Prairies: Discovering the US-Canadian Border*, was published in 1984.

⑮ TOMMY CHANG (*Malaysia*)
Having been a diver for more than 10 years, Chang specialises in underwater photography. Freelancing since 1983 after he left the film unit of Radio Television Malaysia-Sabah — where he was a photographer, cameraman and film editor — Tommy has worked with advertising agencies, travel magazines and book publishers. He participated in the "Eyes on Asean" exhibition in 1992.

⑯ DENNIS LAU (*Malaysia*)
Born and raised in Sarawak, Lau started taking pictures at the age of 13. His intimate knowledge of Sarawak has enabled him to put together a unique photographic record of the environment and its people.

⑰ SLIM SREEDHARAN (*Malaysia*)
A specialist in wildlife photography, Sreedharan is a former journalist and ornithologist who has worked on conservation projects in Africa, India and South-east Asia with the Worldwide Fund for Nature and other similar groups. Now concentrating on documentary films on conservation, he has published four books — *Bako, A Living Museum*, *Humble Beginnings*, *Caught in a Muddle* and *Snakes and Ladders*.

⑱ EMIL V. DAVOCOL (*The Philippines*)
Davocol has had a varied career as a cartoonist, graphic designer, advertising photographer and art director. An active participant in various photographic exhibitions, he has won several national and international photographic awards. Presently he manages his own photography and design studio.

⑲ PETER CHEN (*Singapore*)
A commercial photographer for the last 19 years, Peter's avant-garde style of photography services many commercial and corporate clients worldwide. In 1981, he was conferred a Meritorious Award by the Royal Photographic Society of Great Britain. He operates Chen Shan Company, his studio, in Singapore. He has held two exhibitions locally and has had his work published in *Singapore: Island City State*, a major photographic book on Singapore.

⑳ GERALD GAY (*Singapore*)
A graduate in Fine Arts Photography, Gay began his career practising the craft of still-life photography. A partner of developing Agents Photography since 1986, he has published with Times Editions *The Art of Indonesian Cooking* and *Cuisine Reunionnaise*.

㉑ MUNSHI AHMED (*Singapore*)
A freelance photographer, Ahmed's clients include various commercial and corporate businesses, and regional and international magazines, including *Asiaweek*. His interest is in documentary journalism and industry.

㉒ DOMINIC SANSONI (*Sri Lanka*)
Sansoni was selected by the Arts Council of Great Britain to participate in the "New British Image", an exhibition by young photographers. His pictures can be seen in *Time* and *Asiaweek* and in several inflight magazines. He has published several books on travel and documentary subjects.

㉓ DUANGDAO SUWANARUNGSI (*Thailand*)
With her personal interest in nature, Suwanarungsi has become her country's pre-eminent landscape photographer. She works for the Thai Tourist Authority. Several books of her work have been published, including *Back to the Mountain*, and *Thailand: Seven Days in the Kingdom*.

㉔ PISIT JIROPAS (*Thailand*)
A painter until 12 years ago, Jiropas studied art in Silapakorn University, Bangkok. He has worked on a similar assignment to this book in his native Thailand and was also involved in photographing *Singapore: Island City State*.

㉕ ARA GULER (*Turkey*)
Istanbul-born Guler began his career as a journalist, and after meeting Marc Riboud and Cartier-Bresson, worked on some assignments for Magnum Paris. He went on to be Eastern correspondent for *Life*, *Paris Match* and *Stern*. He has photographed Winston Churchill, Picasso, Salvador Dali and Auguste Renoir. Today, he continues his reportage and portrait photography.

The first chapter opens with a Koranic verse used in everyday life, which means "In the name of Allah, the most Compassionate, the most Merciful".

An elaborate Jawi calligraphic representation of "Brunei Darussalam" decorating the arch of the die-cut design.

Jawi inscription meaning "Darussalam" (Abode of Peace).

1. Kenyah motif from a wood-carving in the collection of the Brunei Museum.

16. Repetition of the Bruneian *bunga telapok berwarna* motif, on contents and appendix pages.

2. Bruneian motif.

17. Motif taken from a songket fabric.

3. Kayan motif from a woodcarving in the Brunei Museum.

18. Islamic design on wall of religious classroom in Brunei.

4. Brunei crest from a *pitis* coin, minted in 1865.

19. Bruneian motif taken from the *usongan*, or royal coronation chariot.

5. Crest, said to date from the reign of Sultan Sharif Ali (1425-1433).

20. Design taken from a tombstone in Royal Mausoleum in Kota Batu, Brunei.

6. A variation on the *air mulih* motif, taken from a brass cannon.

21. Bruneian motif found on the *usongan*, or royal chariot.

7. A medallion based on the *air mulih* motif.

22. Motif on tin-glazed earthernware tile, Tunisia.

8. A quadrafoil *lukut* motif from a Brunei cannon.

23. Arabesque design taken from Koran produced in Cairo in 1304.

9. *Jambangan* leaf motif.

24. Motif on an ornament from Turkey.

10. A single *lukut* leaf motif.

25. 15th century ceramic design from Isfahan, Friday Mosque, Iran.

11. A *bunga jambangan* variation on the *air mulih* form, taken from a Brunei cannon.

26. Inlaid mother-of-pearl, 17th century, Turkey.

12. Modification of *bunga tertai/ bunga melur bersusun* motif.

27. Bronzework, Turkey.

13. Design from an earthenware shard excavated in Kupang, Brunei, dated to about the 10th century.

28. 14th century stucco from mosque of Sidi Bu Medina, Algeria.

14. Motif taken from Royal Mausoleum in Kota Batu, Brunei.

29. Stucco from Mosque of al-Hakim, Cairo, Egypt.

15 Bruneian *air mulih* motif.

30. Bruneian *bunga berantai* motif, on title page.

31. Islamic metalwork design.

32. Hexagonal tile from 15th century mosque at Edirne, Turkey.

33. Palmette detail from a Koran written and illuminated in Iran in 1313.

34. Engraved design from a metal dish cover, c. 1600.

35. Detail from frontispiece of a Koran produced in Iran in 1313.

36. Detail from frontispiece of a Koran produced in Mosul in 1310.

37. Leaf scroll design from frontispiece of Koran produced in Mosul in 1310.

38. Detail from a wooden box with mother-of-pearl inlay, Syria.

39. Leaf scroll from a Koran produced in Cairo in 1304.

40. Seven-circle pottery design common to various parts of the Islamic world.

41. Detail taken from a Bruneian royal shield.

42. Star-and-crescent design from the royal crown worn by the Sultan of Brunei Darussalam.

43. Stylised ornamental leaf form.

44. Palmette leaf scroll inscribed on pottery, 9th-12th centuries.

45. Palmette design painted on dish.

46. Design on silver and copper inlaid tray with Mamluk-style decoration, 19th century Egypt.

47. Design on 13th century large bronze cauldron from Khorasan.

48. Design taken from *usongan*, or royal chariot, Brunei Darussalam.

49. Pinwheel motif decorating the dome of the *Bangunan Alat Kebesaran Di Raja* (Royal Regalia Building).

50. Shell motif.

51. Motif on a Bruneian medal.

52. Bruneian motif taken from *usongan*, or royal chariot.

53. Motif on a Bruneian medal.

54. Bruneian motif on ceremonial shield used during Silver Jubilee procession.

55. Bruneian motif on collar of a chariot bearer during Silver Jubilee procession.

56. Design taken from Bruneian medal.

57. Palmette design of the Sasanian tradition painted on dish.

58. Motif taken from a Bruneian ceremonial shield.

59. Detail from the royal shield, or *perisai kerajaan*.

A
Abode of Peace 22
Abdul Razak Plaza 38
akad nikah 72
agricultural projects 170, 171
agricultural training college
147
armed forces 153, 156
arts 183
Arts and Handicrafts Centre
78, 84
Awang 20
azan 71

B
baju kurong 17
Bandar Seri Begawan 17, 38
*Bangunan Alat Kebesaran
Di Raja* 130 (see also Royal
Regalia Building)
barn swallow 47
Batu Apoi Forest Reserve 38,
57
Begawan Sultan (Blessed
Sultan) 34
bersanding ceremony 78
Bethune, John Drinkwater
17, 33
birth 71
Bornean gibbon 55
'Borneo Proper' 24
bridegroom 24
British Malayan Petroleum
Company 37
British North Borneo
Company 34
British, arrival of the 33-34
Brooke, Charles 34
Brooke, James 30, 33-34
Bruneians 144, 180-181, 186
Brunei Bay 22, 24, 176
Brunei Darussalam, origins
of name 22
Brunei History Centre 26
Brunei Investment Agency
19
Brunei Islamic Trust, The 19,
20
Brunei *kiri* 24
Brunei Liquefied Natural Gas
Plant 34, 37, 164, 166
Brunei Malay Regiment 153
Brunei Malays 24
Brunei Museum 26
Brunei River 17, 22
Brunei Shell Group 37, 164
Brunei Town 26, 30, 33, 34

C
camphor 19, 24
cattle farming 37, 170
ceremonial shields 30
chalak makanan 33
Chinese temple 105
community spirit 17
community life 98
conservation, forest 40, 54
55
crafts, traditional 26, 106

D
dipterocarp forest 51, 57
doa selamat 73

E
economic diversification 37,
173
economic self-sufficiency 37,
170, 173
education 19, 113, 146, 147
ethnic groups 24

F
family life 17
food 189
foreign influences 20
foreign trade 19

G
gas 19, 161
gasing 185
Government 20

H
Hari Raya Puasa 17
Hassanal Bolkiah National
Stadium 185
healthcare 19, 151
history 22, 24, 26, 30, 33, 34
- advent of Islam 26
- arrival of British 33
- British protection 34
- centre of trade 26
- civil war 33
- expansion of empire 30
- Islamic missionary
activity 30, 33
- military power 24
- piracy 33
- renaissance 34
- trading power 24
- visit of Magellan's ships 30
- war with the Spanish 33
housing 176

I
Iban 24, 26, 111
independence 22
international relations 20
Islam 17, 20, 22, 34, 63, 71
- advent of 26
Islamic Bank of Brunei 20,
176
Islamic greeting 17
Islamic law 89
Istana Nurul Iman 22, 40,
126, 195
- Lapau (Royal Ceremonial
Hall) 135
- Throne Room 126, 130,
131, 135

J
jewellery, bridal 26
jewellery, traditional 81
jong sarat 24, 78, 81

K
kadhi 72
Kampong Ayer 17, 22, 30,
33, 94, 98, 99, 106
Kedayan woman 106
ketupat 84, 86
Kris Si Naga 19
Kuala Belalong Field Studies
Centre 38, 57
Kuching Emas 19

L
lesong kayu 33
living standard 19
longhouse 106, 113

M
Makam Di-Raja 30 (see also
Royal Mausoleum)
Malay architecture 30, 106,
195
Malay Muslim Monarchy 19,
22 (see also *Melayu Islam
Beraja*)
mangrove 47
Marco Polo 24
marriage 72, 73
Melayu Islam Beraja 19
Ministry of Industry and
Primary Resources 37
mu'ezzin 17
Muja 26
Murut woman 111
Mushaf Brunei Darussalam
20
*Mushaf Universiti Brunei
Darussalam* 138
music, traditional 82

N
Nakhoda Ragam 30
National Development Plans
173, 176
national identity 19
National Flag 19
nipah palm 47
'nodding donkeys' 37

O
oil 19, 37
- discovery of 34, 37
oil and gas industry 34, 37,
162-163
offshore operations 161, 169
Omar Ali Saifuddien Mosque
20, 22, 63, 68

P
Padang Berawa 37
Pangangun 77
papat jambol 71
Pehins 20
Penan 24, 26, 113
Prince Azim 136
Prince Al-Muhtadee Billah
20, 136
Prince Jefri 136
Prince Mohamed 136
Princess Rashidah 139
Prince Sufri 136
pengirans 24, 26
P'oni 24
Pusat Sejarah 26

R
Radio Television Brunei 190
rain forest 38, 47, 51, 52
recreation 185
redshanks 47
religious activity 68, 89
religious education 22, 63
religious freedom 33
religious tolerance 105
Royal Brunei Airlines 38, 174

Royal Brunei Armed Forces
153
royal dynasty 19
Royal Mausoleum 30
royal regalia 19, 22, 130
Royal Regalia Building 130,
193

S
sago 111
Salasilah 26
schooling 148
sepak takraw 185
Shariah Court 89
silat 185
sinjiang 78
songkok 17, 186
spice trade 24, 33
sports 185
Sribuza 26
St Andrew's church 105
stilt houses 94
Sultan Abdul Kahar 30
Sultan Abdul Mumin 34
Sultan Ahmad Tajuddin 34
Sultan Berkat 26
Sultan Bolkiah 30
Sultan Haji Hassanal Bolkiah
19, 22, 118
- coronation 19, 22
- leadership style 20
- Silver Jubilee celebrations
20, 124, 135, 192
Sultan Haji Omar Ali
Saifuddien III 34
Sultan Mohammad Shah 26
Sultan Omar Ali Saifuddin II
30, 33
Sultan Saiful Rijal 33
Sultan Sharif Ali 26

T
*Tabung Amanah Islam
Brunei* 19, 20
Taman Haji Sir Muda Omar
Ali Saifuddien 20, 22
Tamu Kianggeh market 84,
189
Tasek Merimbun 17, 51
Temburong district 47, 52,
57
Temburong River 51
tikar rotan 86
Tongkat Ajai 19
tudong 17
Tutong Mosque 89

U
Universiti Brunei Darussalam
19, 38, 138

V
vocational and technical
training 147

W
Waqaf Mosque 20, 40, 68
water taxis 94
- making of 82
weaving 82
wedding costume 77
wedding festivities 74, 77
wudhu 63

Brunei Darussalam, A Guide (Brunei Shell, Brunei Darussalam, 1992).
Compiled primarily for the staff and visitors of Brunei Shell, this guide offers a colourful and up-to-date introduction to the country's history, geography and cultural life.

Brunei Darussalam in Profile (Government of Brunei Darussalam Publication, London, 1988).
An official publication giving a concise introduction to the political, social and economic structure of modern Brunei Darussalam.

Brunei Darussalam, the Land and its People (Brunei Shell, Brunei Darussalam, 1978; second edition 1984).
The second edition of this pictorial essay on the people and culture of Brunei Darussalam takes the story up to the resumption of the nation's independence in 1984.

The Brunei Museum Journal (Brunei Museum, Brunei Darussalam, 1989).
The Brunei Museum, whose annual journal has appeared since 1969, publishes a wealth of research on all aspects of Bruneian history, particularly in the fields of culture, tradition and art.

Peter Blundell, *The City of Many Waters* (J.W. Arrowsmith, London, 1923).
The author was an employee of a cutch manufacturing company in Brunei Darussalam in the early 1900s. His book provides a sympathetic account of his long residence in the country, particularly interesting for his account of his friendship with Sultan Hashim.

D.E. Brown, *Brunei: the Structure and History of a Bornean Malay Sultanate* (Brunei Museum Monograph, Brunei Darussalam, 1970).
A classic analysis of the historical factors that have formed the complex social and political structure of present-day Brunei Darussalam.

Lord Chalfont, *By God's Will: A Portrait of the Sultan of Brunei* (Weidenfeld and Nicolson, London, 1989).
A biography of the present Sultan of Brunei Darussalam set in the context of the country's modern political development, both domestically and on the international stage.

G.C. Harper, *The Discovery and Development of the Seria Oilfield* (Brunei Museum Monograph, Brunei Darussalam, 1975; second edition 1990).
A detailed historical account of the fascinating story of the growth of Brunei Darussalam's oil industry.

(Ed) Robert Nicholl, *European Sources for the History of the Sultanate of Brunei in the Sixteenth Century* (Brunei Museum, Brunei Darussalam, 1975).
This monograph gathers together all important early references to Brunei in European documents, and builds up a picture of the country's wealth and importance in the fifteenth century.

Spenser St John, *Life in the Forests of the Far East* (2 vols, London, 1862; reprinted Oxford University Press, 1986).
St John's account of his adventures contains a long and valuable account of Brunei in the second half of the nineteenth century.

D.S. Ranjit Singh, *Brunei 1839-1983: The Problems of Political Survival* (Oxford University Press, Singapore, 1984).
A modern scholarly account of the development of Brunei Darussalam.

Wong Khoon Meng, *In Brunei Forests: An introduction to the Plant Life of Brunei Darussalam* (Forestry Department, Brunei Darussalam, 1990).
A beautifully illustrated volume which explores the unique diversity of Brunei Darussalam's forest environment and also describes present conservation measures.